Land and Natural Development (LAND) Code

Land and Natural Development (LAND) Code

Guidelines for Sustainable Land Development

Diana Balmori and Gaboury Benoit

BICENTENNIAL
1807
WILEY
2007
BICENTENNIAL

John Wiley & Sons, Inc.

Library of Congress Cataloging-in-Publication Data:

Balmori, Diana.
   Land and natural development (LAND) code : guidelines for sustainable land development. / Diana Balmori, Gaboury Benoit.
      p. cm.
   "Published simultaneously in Canada."
   Includes bibliographical references.
   ISBN 978-0-470-04984-6 (cloth : alk. paper)
   1. Real estate development—Environmental aspects—United States. 2. Land use—Environmental aspects—United States.   3. Building—Environmental aspects—United States. 4. Sustainable development—United States.   I. Benoit, Gaboury.   II. Title.
   HD255.B34 2007
   333.77—dc22   2006027160

Printed in the United States of America

10 9 8 7 6 5 4 3 2 1

Contents

Acknowledgments

This book is intended primarily for design professionals, such as architects, landscape architects, urban planners, and urban designers, as well as civil engineers and developers. It originated at Yale University, as a unique collaboration in the study of landscape design and forestry. Professor Emeritus Herb Bormann inspired this document, bringing Gaboury Benoit and Diana Balmori together to think about guidelines for sustainable development of land. The two authors had equal, if unique, roles in preparing the book; they are listed alphabetically.

Colleen Murphy-Dunning organized and ran the original research seminar that served as the nucleus for this book. A prodigious organizer for this very complex course she juggled outside speakers, in-house critics, and constant adjustments in the subjects in response to reviews and research. Her energy and intelligence were critical to being able to pull this all together into the LAND Code.

We thank developer Ned Foss and his partner Lawrence Linder of CGI & Partners in Delmar, New York, and Margery Groten, Senior Project Manager of Scenic Hudson, the organization that is developing in a sustainable manner with CGI & Partners. They gave of their time and arranged for us to visit the property they are developing in Beacon, New York. This property served as an initial base for the students' work.

We thank very specifically our dedicated graduate students who worked with enthusiasm and seriousness on this uncharted terrain. One or two of them researched and were responsible for each of the topics we laid out for the code. Their work was the kernel for the School of Forestry and

Environmental Studies (SFES) Working Paper that followed and served as the seed for this book. We also would like to thank the many top-notch scholars in each of the specialties this document contains (hydrology, law, etc.), who lectured on the state of the art in their discipline and answered questions by the student team assigned to the topic. In the latter part of the semester, they also critiqued the first summaries of the work of the student teams.

We are grateful, too, for the financial support given to this work by the Hixon Center for Urban Ecology at the Yale School of Forestry & Environmental Studies. A research and outreach organization, Hixon Center objectives are principally pursued through four center programs: the Urban Resources Initiative, the Urban Watershed Program, Public-Private Partnerships for the Urban Environment, and the Program for Sustainable Environmental Design. This course fit the objectives of all the center's programs.

Distinguished Guest Lecturers

Russell Albanese, President, Albanese Development Corporation, Garden City, New York, Developer of the Solaire Building, the first New York City building to be assigned under the new Battery Park City environmental guidelines

Clinton Andrews, Associate Professor, E.J. Bloustein School of Planning and Public Policy, Rutgers University, President, IEEE Society on Social Implications of Technology

Wendi Goldsmith, President and Senior Bioengineer and Geomorphologist, the Bioengineering Group, Inc., Salem, Massachusetts

James Lima, Senior Vice President, Special Projects Division NYC Economic Development Corporation

Ruben Lubowski, Natural Resource Economist, USDA

Edward G. Mitchell, Assistant Professor, Yale School of Architecture

John Nolon, Professor of Law, Pace University Law School. Director, Land Use Law Center

Rafael Pelli, Architect of Solaire Building, New York City

Jonathan Rose, Developer

Tom Schueler, Director of Watershed Research and Practice, Center for Watershed Protection, Ellicott City, Maryland

Yale Faculty and Outside Experts

Erin Mansur and Paul Fisette—Energy
Mark Ashton and Herb Bormann—Ecology
Marian Chertow, Clinton Andrews, and Steven Peck—Industrial Ecology
Jim MacBroom and Wendi Goldsmith—Environmental Engineering
Sheila Olmstead and Ruben Lubowski—Economics, Finance
John Nolon—Law
Gaboury Benoit and Tom Schueler—Hydrology
Jonathan Rose and Russell Albanese—Development
James Lima—Government
Diana Balmori—Design

Student Research Teams

Hydrology and Water Quality
Marni Burns
Beth Owen

Air/Micrometeorology
Cherie LeBlanc

Living Resources
Rosemarie Mannik

Energy
Florence Miller
Carla Short

Environmental Engineering
Christopher Menone
Terrence Miller

Industrial Ecology
William Pott
Elizabeth Roberts

Legal Strategies
Melanie Cutler
William Finnegan

Saving Time and Money
Loni Gardner
Brian Goldberg

Land and Natural Development (LAND) Code

chapter 1

Introduction

WHAT THIS BOOK IS ABOUT

The Land and Natural Development (LAND) Code is a research-based guide to ecologically sound land development intended for architects, engineers, landscape architects, developers, city officials, students, and interested individuals. Our goal in creating the LAND Code has been to delineate a clear and practical pathway for developing sites in harmony with natural processes. Land *will* be developed, and this manual shows how that can be done with the least environmental harm. That does not necessarily mean leaving nature alone; sometimes the best results can be achieved with intensively engineered methods. Nevertheless, we try to recommend ways that natural processes can be partly retained or re-created by the use of engineered structures and practices that emulate the natural processes they supplant. These engineered methods cover the gamut from vegetated rain gardens to storage tanks, which gather and reuse drainage water for irrigation or other nonpotable uses. The engineered solution needs to be close in its workings to the natural process it supplants. Each kind of site will require treatment appropriate to its nature and context, and the LAND Code is suited to many kinds of land uses, from greenfields to redeveloped urban brownfields to converted farmlands.

WHY THIS BOOK

Readers may ask: Why the LAND Code? Don't other recent "green" or sustainable guidelines already provide guidance for environmentally sound land development? Many of the principles of the LAND Code do appear in the U.S. Environmental Protection Agency (EPA) recommendations and in the Leadership in Energy and Environmental Design (LEED) Green Building Council rating system. But the LAND Code has several unique characteristics:

- It has a rigorous scientific basis. LAND draws heavily and almost exclusively on peer-reviewed scientific research to derive its recommendations. Other systems are much more the product of expert judgment.

- It provides a rating scheme that strives to weight each practice according to the scale of its environmental benefit and the difficulty of it implementation. LEED, by comparison, gives 1 point to nearly every recommendation no matter how beneficial and costly.

- It is nearly self-contained. LAND does not rely on several voluminous and complicated external protocols (e.g., the ASTM E1903–97 "Phase II Environmental Site Assessment"; the EPA 832/R-92–005 "Storm Water Management for Construction Activities," Chapter 3; or the EPA-840-B-92–002 "Guidance Specifying Management Measures for Sources of Nonpoint Pollution in Coastal Waters"). Instead, the LAND Code provides a simple and straightforward step-by-step system. Most of its recommendations can be carried out by nonexperts, especially on smaller sites.

- It is comprehensive, covering water, soil, air, energy, materials, and living resources.

- It focuses on the land, not on buildings.

- It makes extensive use of illustrations, both photographs and diagrams, to make many issues clear and understandable.

LAND also can be used readily in conjunction with LEED, EPA, or other guidelines. Perhaps the most important difference between LAND and other documents is the explicit reliance on scientific studies as the basis for its recommendations. It uses the latest research about natural processes and engineering methods; thus, it will necessarily be an evolving document. The field of sustainability is quite new, and its science will continue to reveal new truths about natural processes, which LAND will need to incorporate over time.

HOW TO USE THIS BOOK

The core of the text consists of seven major subject areas that are critical to developing land sustainably: water, soil, air, living resources, energy, and materials. These are followed by a seventh, environmental engineering methods, which presents technical information about some of the tools that are available to achieve sustainable results. At the risk of oversimplifying the distinction, this last chapter deals more directly with urban sites where development density often prevents "natural" bioengineered systems from being constructed. The other chapters place somewhat greater emphasis on less intensively developed lands, whether forests, greenfields, or farmland, where more space is available. Another way of looking at the first six chapters compared to the seventh is that the earlier ones provide recommendations to achieve sustainable development based on scientific research on natural processes. The seventh describes a tool-box of material ways and means to get there.

At the end of the book, Chapter 9, " Different Paths to Sustainability," gives case studies of development projects that aim for sustainability and that have been recently built or are underway now. The projects have been chosen to provide snapshots of a variety of approaches to green development, as well as some specific examples where one of the six main topics (water, soil, air, energy, materials, living resources) has been addressed successfully. The case studies vary in length according to the complexity of the examples—that is, on how many fronts the project has features relevant to our guide. In some, the structuring of the development group may be the point of the example (e.g., the partnership of one developer with a conservation group, Scenic Hudson Inc., to give the green agenda a more prominent place in the development project). In others, it may be how sustainable approaches were used to allow a regional mall developer to build upstream from a water supply reservoir, with benefits to both the developer and the water utility. The examples given in this last section, therefore, give a quick overview of the very fast-growing field of sustainable land development. They are there to demonstrate that real projects succeed at developing land sustainably.

HOW LAND CODE POINTS WERE DETERMINED

It was clear that a rating scheme would greatly increase this book's utility to the user. But how do you compare the environmental benefit of a constructed wetland to that of full cutoff light fixtures or proximity to mass transit? One approach is to simply assign one point to every action, but, clearly, the benefits of some measures are much greater than others. On the other hand, fully understanding the relative environmental value of each strategy might take years of research and still not yield clear answers. Consequently, we opted for a hybrid system that relates points to total benefits, but doesn't require unrealistically detailed knowledge of ecosystem structure and function. Part of the answer came when we struggled to assign each strategy to single areas of environmental benefit (water, soil, air quality, energy, etc.). Some measures (e.g., retaining mature trees on a site) provide gains in almost every category, whereas others (e.g., providing bike racks) narrowly benefit only one or two. It seemed reasonable to provide a point for each environmental subsystem or function that is protected by a given recommended structure or activity.

Furthermore, some measures are much easier or cheaper to implement than others, and the difficult and expensive ones need to be rewarded, or they will never be implemented. Points are, therefore, awarded for difficulty. Also, some recommended actions have lasting effect, whereas others are temporary or uncertain in their long-term benefit. A point is awarded to any strategy whose effect is probably permanent. Finally, there are some activities that are so clearly necessary that developing land sustainably is impossible without them. These are not given points, but are simply required.

Once the various recommendations had been assigned points by this system, they were sorted by point value and checked for internal consistency. The criterion applied was whether recommendations in a given part of the ranking seemed to provide equivalent environmental benefit. We were gratified to find that the relative number of points were reasonable and required no further adjustment.

The LAND Code has three levels of achievement: silver, gold, and platinum. These three are awarded for achieving 40 to 60 percent, 60 to 80 percent, or 80 to 100 percent, respectively, of the possible total points at a given site. The maximum attainable point total varies from site to site, and this total needs to be calculated along with the number of LAND points awarded. As an example, it is not possible to create migration passageways under roads on sites without roads, so these points should not be included when calculating the achievable maximum for such sites.

Furthermore, in some instances LAND points are awarded for mitigating the effect of what amounts to poor site selection. Examples include leaving buffer zones around sensitive aquatic ecosystems, such as streams, wetlands, and vernal pools. To avoid perverse incentives, selecting sites with such features triggers the awarding of negative LAND points, which can be canceled partially or entirely through mitigation measures.

Conceptually, using precious metals to signify achievement is antithetical to the spirit of the LAND Code, as these metals are scarce natural resources whose extraction cause severe environmental damage (De Lacerda 2003; Muezzinoglu 2003). Nevertheless, we could think of no environmentally benign trio of substances or objects whose hierarchical ranking is so obvious, and no actual environmental harm is done in awarding these categories.

HOW WE USE THE TERM *SUSTAINABILITY*

Our use of *sustainability* applies exclusively to the environmental aspects of land development. Although economic development and social organization are considered, they are secondary. This text is concerned with natural conditions and their continuity over time; our goal is to keep the long term in the development equation.

Probably the most commonly articulated expression of sustainability is that of the U.N. World Commission in a 1987 report on Environment and Development (WCED) from the publication "Our Common Future." The publication is also known as the "Brundtland Report," and states that sustainable development "meets the needs of the present without compromising the ability of future generations to meet their own needs." While we agree with this definition, its focus is on people, the "generations," rather than the environment; therefore, we adhere more closely the EPA's definition: "the ability of an ecosystem to maintain a defined/desired state of ecological integrity over time."

In this text, we address environmental aspects of land development. We focus on natural systems and processes that are altered by land use, and seek ways for their functions to be aided or replaced by engineered elements for long-term protection of ecosystems. We believe environmental sustainability furthers human sustainability by creating systems that add to people's comfort, enjoyment, and health.

We have also considered aesthetics as part of the broader agenda, for it contributes greatly to people's attachment to a place, an important prerequisite for sustainability. For a time, it seemed most ecological projects were badly designed aesthetically, and only recently has an effort emerged to get them both right. Therefore, we have made an effort—particularly in the case studies presented in the last section—to choose examples that are both environmentally sustainable and well designed.

HOW THIS BOOK CAME ABOUT

The research for this book was first issued as a Yale School of Forestry and Environmental Studies working paper in order to open up a dialogue and benefit from the insights and experience of its readers. Based on responses to this first document and the opportunity to publish it as a technical manual offered by John Wiley & Sons, Inc., a new text has been written with more thorough development of its topics and additional illustrations clarifying and visually informing the text. And because, in general, science publications have traditionally paid little attention to illustrations and their aesthetic quality, a special effort has been made to heed to the saying that a picture is worth a thousand words. To that end, the illustrations attempt to make the recommended sustainable actions and methods clear and understandable at a glance, as well as being well composed.

The LAND Code grew out of a course taught by faculty members, Gaboury Benoit of the Yale School of Forestry and Environmental Studies, and Diana Balmori of the Yale School of Architecture. The course, "Natural Development: Towards Certification of New Uses of Green and Brownfields," was a graduate seminar in which students were divided into teams to research eight topics decided on by the instructors, with the help of Colleen Murphy-Dunning, program director of the Hixon Center for Urban Ecology. The eight topics were: Water Quality and Hydrology, Air Pollution and Micrometeorology, Plant Ecology and Population/Community Ecology, On-site Energy and Transportation, Industrial Ecology, Environmental Engineering, Legal Strategies for Municipalities and Developers, and Saving Time and Money. The course offered a rich mix of outside specialists who lectured on the eight selected topics. In-house specialists and the course's two teachers critiqued the students' research as it proceeded.

In its evolution from a series of research papers to a text for a broader audience, some topics were subdivided and others eliminated. In particular, soils were given greater prominence, water quality and hydrology were individually given greater prominence, and legal strategies were dropped because they would need a whole volume in themselves. The entire text has been extensively reorganized and rewritten.

Water

SITE DRAINAGE

The flow of water is just as important to an ecosystem as circulation of blood is to the human body. Water carries nutrients in and waste out, modulates temperature, sculpts the landscape, provides habitat, and facilitates reproduction and growth of countless organisms both aquatic and terrestrial. All of these critical functions can be impaired through human alteration of the landscape that takes place when land is developed.

Modern thinking on how to handle drainage has turned 180 degrees from earlier approaches. In the past, the goal was to collect rainwater and move it off the site as quickly as possible. This requires substantial site disturbance and installation of costly infrastructure. Any treatment to improve water quality had to occur at the end of the pipe, but was more often simply neglected. Stormwater was treated essentially as a waste product. Paradoxically, landowners pay for systems to remove water from their property and pay again to import water to use on their land. The modern approach, embodied in systems like low-impact development (LID), is to slow water as it passes across and through the landscape, to retain it in natural or constructed water features, to allow as much as possible to drain into soils or evaporate to the atmosphere, and then to release as little as possible, as slowly as feasible, downstream. Water is viewed as a resource to be saved and used. This approach requires treatment of water at the source, at numerous locations distributed across the landscape—often for less money—and produces cleaner more measured flows in receiving streams.

Minimizing the environmental impact of development requires careful, commonsense planning. From the standpoint of the hydrologic cycle, this means evaluating the natural and built elements of the site and how they will interact with water. Are surface water features present, such as streams, lakes, wetlands, or vernal pools? What is the slope of the land, and are there any very steep slopes that are vulnerable to erosion? Will water naturally flow onto the site from elsewhere? Are soils well or poorly drained? Where will water naturally flow within the site, and where does it ultimately drain after it leaves? What is the local climate like, and how often does it rain—2 inches, 4 inches, or 6 inches? All of these questions are easily answered

Water moves through the earth's atmosphere, land, surface water, and groundwater in a continuous cycle with no definable start or finish. *Daniel R. Abdo. Adapted from Federal Interagency Stream Restoration Working Group.*

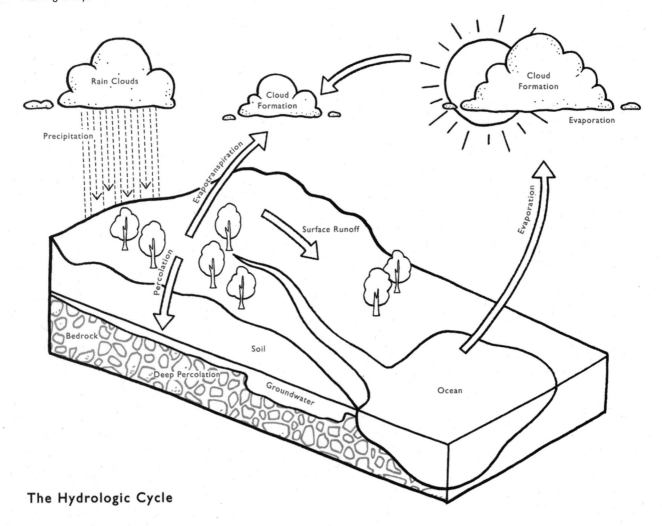

The Hydrologic Cycle

through a site visit and with information readily available on the Internet and elsewhere.

The drainage plan divides the landscape into a series of patches, which are ideally subwatersheds. The water yield from each of these elements is determined, and a strategy is devised to slow movement of water across the landscape, to encourage infiltration into soils and evaporation to the atmosphere, and to minimize the amount of water that passes out of each subwatershed. Typically, the measures used are low cost, low maintenance, and similar to natural landscape elements; however, site constraints may make it necessary to use conventional engineering measures (cisterns, pipes, culverts, etc.). The drainage plan narrative benefits from two technical aids: maps and models.

All of the features that influence the retention and flow of water should be drawn on a map. This can be simple or complex, depending on the scope of the project in question. A sketch would suffice for a single house lot, whereas a detailed topographical map prepared by a surveyor would be needed for large developments, such as housing projects or shopping centers. Geographic information system (GIS) software provides the ultimate mapping capability, but requires considerable technical skill, and is beyond the needs of all but the most complex development projects.

Modeling is another powerful aid in the process of developing a drainage plan. Fortunately, hydrologic modeling can be relatively easy, as the behavior of water is straightforward: it always flows downhill. How quickly it flows depends on characteristics with which we are all familiar, including slope and the type of surface (e.g., pavement, grass, forest). The data needed for hydrologic models (e.g., rainfall intensities, soil characteristics) are readily available in reference books, online, or as lookup tables within the models themselves. Anyone who can balance a checkbook can use the Rational Method (Maidment 1993) to quantify and predict site drainage. Slightly more complicated are models such as TR-55 (National Resource Conservation Service), but anyone who has filled out a Federal 1040 form should find these models easy to apply. Both of these models are available for free download; and interactive websites are also available (e.g., www.geocities.com/Eureka/Concourse/ 3075/rational.html). More complicated still are models such as the U.S. Environmental Protection Agency's (EPA's) Hydrological Simulation Program—Fortran (HSPF) and Storm Water Management Model (SWMM), which can include both water quantity and quality calculations. These two models are probably best suited to large development projects where engineering consultants are usually employed. Increasingly, the methods used in these several models can be linked to GIS software to carry out calculations in a spatially

Designing with, not against, a site's natural hydrology is an effective and cost-efficient way to deal with site drainage issues. *Photos by Catherine Byun and Kira Appelhans.*

explicit framework (Djokic and Maidment 1993). Whatever the size and complexity of the project, modeling is a useful tool.

Together, the drainage map, modeling, and drainage plan provide a framework within which to develop the site. The drainage plan should mesh with strategies to safeguard water quality, protect soils, and conserve biodiversity (see later chapters). Fortunately, all of these goals support each other and follow from designing with nature. A number of resources are available to assist developers in preparing drainage plans. These include free downloadable publications from the EPA (Prince George's County Maryland Department of Environmental Resources, 1999; Bay Area Stormwater Management Agencies Association (BASMAA), 1999; and Center for Watershed Protection (CWP), www.cwp.org, 2003). The importance of treating runoff at its source cannot be overemphasized. The flows from just a few untreated developed sites quickly combine to form a torrent that may be impossible to control (Kochel et al. 2005) except through the use of massive and costly engineered structures (e.g., channel armoring) with serious ecosystem impacts. Reducing and treating flows near their source emulates natural hydrologic controls and allows downstream water conveyances to have a lower cost and smaller environmental footprint.

Recommendation

Understand the flow of water into, through, and off the site, and prepare maps, models, and a narrative drainage plan. The goal is to make the system function as closely as possible to predevelopment conditions. One benchmark is to design the site to maintain or restore drainage patterns and channel storage capacity to accommodate flow from a 24-hour storm with a five-year recurrence interval (i.e., a 20 percent probability of occurrence in any given year).

Developer Benefits

- Provision of aesthetically appealing surface water features and open space.

- Cheaper water conveyances than engineered in-ground systems.

- Less frequent maintenance and lower maintenance costs.

- Reduction of flood risk and liability.

Floods are classified according to their frequency and depth. A 25-year flood has a 1-in-25 chance of occurring in any given year. A 100-year flood, though less frequent, is more destructive. *Daniel R. Abdo. Adapted from Roy Deguisti and http://collections.ic.gc.ca/streams.*

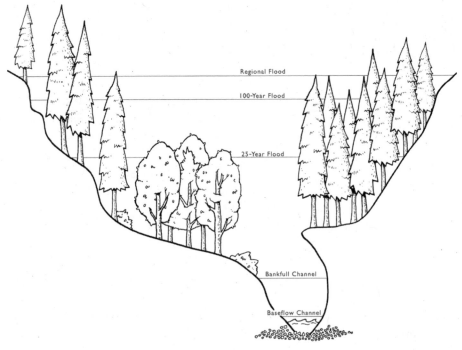

Storm Hydrograph

- Easier achievement of National Pollutant Discharge Elimination System (NPDES) Stormwater Phase II and Total Maximum Daily Load (TMDL) permits.

- More physically comfortable and aesthetically appealing environment as a result of evapotranspiration cooling the air in summer.

Ecosystem Benefits

- Less destructive flood flows.

- Higher flows during dry periods.

- Better water quality.

- Aquatic habitat protection.

- Promotion of biodiversity by quality habitat, provided by diverse drainage features.

Strategies

- Use simple hydrologic models first to quantify how water flows originally, and second to predict how flows will respond to development plans on-site: ***Required.***

- Map the site's predevelopment hydrologic features, including slopes, flow paths, soil types, and vegetation: ***Required.***

- Prepare a drainage plan narrative with the goal of matching postdevelopment water movement as closely as possible to predevelopment conditions. The plan should explain how to slow water and allow maximal infiltration and evapotranspiration: ***Required.***

Grass-lined swales and water channels capture water from storm events to prevent flooding and to slow water velocity, allowing for water infiltration and purification. *William F. Hunt III, North Carolina State University.*

Constructed wetlands can be integrated into industrial hardscapes to capture and treat stormwater on-site. *Michael Van Valkenburgh Associates Inc.*

Drainage features on the site should be designed to accommodate a 24-hour storm with a five-year recurrence interval. Selecting the five-year storm reflects a compromise between handling short recurrence events, which contribute the vast majority of aggregate water volume (because of their frequency), and low-frequency events responsible for major flooding. For much of the eastern United States, a five-year storm delivers only about 25 percent more water than a two-year storm, whereas a 50-year storm represents only a 50 percent increment above a five-year storm (U.S. Soil Conservation Service 1986).

• Follow drainage plan and use bioengineered structures, such as open vegetated spaces, swales, check dams, and rain gardens, to reduce volume and slow velocity of water within drainageway to rates that match predevelopment values based on modeling studies: *12 points.*

Design development to preserve existing drainage patterns on an undeveloped site; or design to create open vegetated spaces and restore historical drainage patterns for previously developed sites.

• Preserve the natural contour of the site, except to produce swales, rain gardens, and detention areas that mimic natural topography: *12 points.*

Extensive regrading of sites is one of the worst causes of interference with natural drainage patterns. Existing landforms reflect equilibrium of

Rocks and vegetation provide roughness that slows down water, allowing sediments to settle out as it moves through the wetland. *Courtesy of the Philadelphia Water Department.*

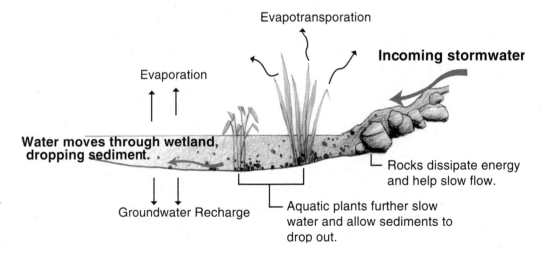

natural forces established on the site over millennia. Leaving the original contour also is enormously effective in protecting soils and preventing erosion.

- Where new drainage structures must be installed, immediately stabilize new channels with vegetation, live stakes, live mats, or other means (see Chapter 8, "Environmental Engineering"): *5 points.*

   This measure is also critically important for preventing erosion.

- For heavily developed urban sites with inadequate space for bioengineered solutions, capture all the stormwater volume for up to a 24-hour storm having a five-year recurrence interval and either reuse it for irrigation or other purposes, or time and meter its release at a rate that will not exceed baseflow levels: [*10 points* (under Water Conservation and Reuse)].

- Incorporate vegetated setbacks that are at least 100 feet (33 meters) wide from all open waterways: [*10 points* (under Buffer Critical Habitat)].

   Setbacks allow adequate slowing and filtration of runoff before drainage reaches channels. They are also critical for protecting habitat

Check dams slow down the flow of water during storm events, increasing water infiltration and reducing erosion. *Courtesy of Gove Environmental Services, Exeter, New Hampshire.*

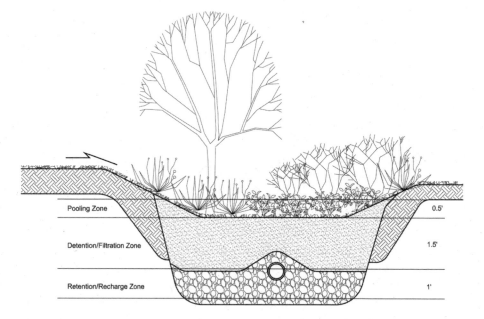

Pooling Zone — 0.5'

Detention/Filtration Zone — 1.5'

Retention/Recharge Zone — 1'

When it rains, water initially pools in the garden's top layer with the plants, percolating quickly from there down to lower layers of infiltration. *Balmori Associates. Adapted from Zolna Russell, Landscape Architect.*

Rain gardens, such as this one near a school, are both bioretention sites, to capture stormwater, and attractive gardens for humans and wildlife. *Reprinted with permission by Kieser and Associates, Inc., Kalamazoo, Michigan.*

and removing contaminants. Continuous forested riparian buffers are emerging as one of the most important elements for protecting aquatic ecosystems (Moore and Palmer 2005).

IMPERVIOUS SURFACES

Imperviousness poses a serious threat to aquatic ecosystems. Water washing off roofs and pavement has higher levels of contaminants, and flows with greater destructive force, than if it passed slowly through soils. A recent study indicates that 44,000 square miles (113,00 square kilometers) of land in the United States are currently covered with impervious surface (Elvidge et al. 2004), similar in area to the state of Ohio. Notably, this is not the area of land with a significant proportion of impervious surface, but the sum of all the truly impervious surface area. Because the proportion of imperviousness in developed land is thought to average about 25 percent, the amount of urbanized land amounts to an area about the size of Pennsylvania, Ohio, Virginia,

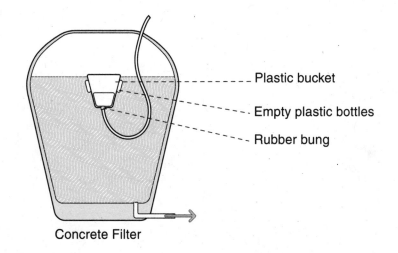

Plastic bucket

Empty plastic bottles

Rubber bung

Concrete Filter

Instead of entering sewers that go directly to open water, rainwater can be captured from roofs, stored in tanks, and filtered with simple devices for irrigation or other on-site uses. *Balmori Associates. Adapted from C. M. Way and T. H. Thomas, 2005.*

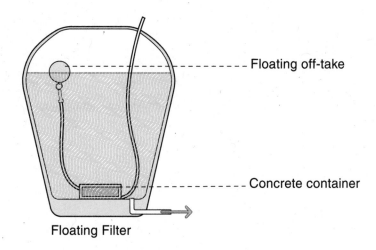

Floating off-take

Concrete container

Floating Filter

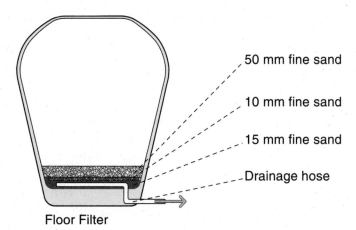

50 mm fine sand

10 mm fine sand

15 mm fine sand

Drainage hose

Floor Filter

TANK STORAGE AND FILTER SYSTEMS

A buffer protects this river from the impacts of agriculture and development, promoting its hydrologic and ecological functions. *Department of Natural Resource Ecology and Management, Iowa State University.*

and Tennessee combined. Expressed another way, this is greater than the combined area of the 12 smallest states.

The natural water cycle begins with rain and snow falling on the landscape. This water follows several pathways, with some filtering into soils, some slaking the water needs of plants, some evaporating back to the atmosphere, and some running off the land's surface into streams. For healthy functioning ecosystems, the last pathway should be the smallest, with typically less than 10 percent of precipitation flowing directly to streams, lakes, and rivers. Water that returns to the atmosphere via physical evaporation and biologically mediated transpiration renews the hydrologic cycle. Water that passes through soils and groundwater aquifers receives natural filtration and biological cleansing. This water also seeps into streams gradually, providing flow during dry periods and avoiding flooding when it is wet. Water that runs across the surface receives little filtration and biological cleansing, is not available to plants, and causes streams and rivers to swell quickly and, sometimes, destructively.

Many characteristics influence the balance among the various pathways of the hydrologic cycle. These factors include the steepness of the land, the characteristics of soils, the nature and extent of plant communities, and human alterations to the landscape. Replacing porous soils with hard, impervious surfaces, such as roofs, roads, and parking lots, causes a greater proportion of water to flow rapidly to streams, picking up contaminants, causing erosion, destroying aquatic habitat, and eradicating sensitive organisms. The proportion of impervious surface is a landscape characteristic that is both intuitive and very easily measurable, and it turns out to be a remarkably powerful predictor of potential damage to aquatic ecosystems. Literally hundreds of scientific studies have shown that imperviousness is linked to elevated flood flows, increased pollution levels, enhanced channel erosion, accelerated

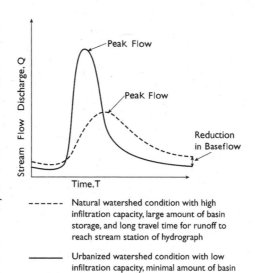

Natural watershed condition with high infiltration capacity, large amount of basin storage, and long travel time for runoff to reach stream station of hydrograph

Urbanized watershed condition with low infiltration capacity, minimal amount of basin storage, and short travel time for runoff to reach stream station of hydrograph

Urban watersheds are "flashier" than natural ones, characterized by sudden, high volumes of flow. Undeveloped watersheds have a less extreme flow range. *Balmori Associates. Adapted from Ohio Department of Natural Resources.*

habitat destruction, and augmented loss of species diversity (research summarized in: Center for Watershed Protection 2003; Paul and Meyer 2001). Many of the studies—and common sense—indicate that imperviousness actually causes the negative environmental consequences; they are not merely correlated with each other. The connection between impervious surface area and damage to aquatic ecosystems has been very well studied, and all of the research supports the same conclusions.

Interestingly, the environmental harm caused by imperviousness does not increase in a simple way in proportion to area; it accelerates dramatically. Specifically, there appears to be a threshold near 10 percent imperviousness where environmental damage increases precipitously (Booth and Jackson 1997). Beyond 25 to 30 percent imperviousness, environmental damage tends to level off, but largely because aquatic ecosystems are so severely degraded that there is little room for further decline. For comparison, residential land use with 2-acre lots typically has 12 percent imperviousness, whereas zones with 1/4-acre lots have close to 30 percent imperviousness. Heavily developed retail, industrial, and office areas generally exceed 80 percent impervious surface (Brabec et al. 2002).

It is because of the well-established relationship between impervious surface area and damage to aquatic ecosystems that our central recommendation is to develop sites so that they emulate conditions with no more than 10 percent impervious surface area. This can be accomplished through a variety of

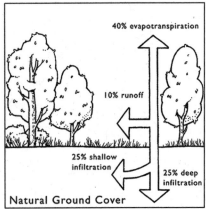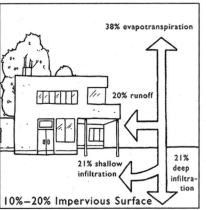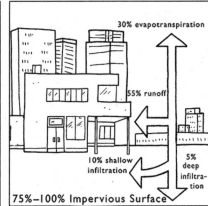

Relationship between impervious cover and surface runoff
Urban Hydrologic Cycle

Urbanization decreases infiltration and increases runoff. As little as 10 percent impervious cover can have a major impact on local streams. *Daniel R. Abdo. Adapted from Federal Interagency Stream Restoration Working Group.*

strategies and does not limit actual imperviousness to 10 percent. Disconnecting impervious surfaces from storm drains, substituting pervious paving materials for impervious ones, using green roofs, and draining parking areas to rain gardens all work as effectively as more direct methods, such as smaller parking lots and narrower roads.

Reducing effective imperviousness and designing hydrologic systems in balance with nature have become increasingly easy to implement. A variety of resources are available to aid developers, and new products come on the market every year. This approach is becoming mainstream under design systems such as LID, which is promoted by organizations as diverse as the EPA and the American Society of Civil Engineers (ASCE).

Two caveats are worth noting that relate to the value of limiting impervious surfaces. First, few studies have been conducted in arid parts of the United States, and these regions have hydrologic cycles that differ in important ways from more humid sections. However, at least one study from an arid North American location supports restricting imperviousness (Janeau et al. 1999). Lacking evidence to the contrary, it seems prudent to recommend limiting imperviousness even in dry locations.

The second stipulation relates to the scale of benefit. There is no question that imperviousness causes environmental damage. However, so far there have been few studies providing empirical evidence that application of management practices that ameliorate imperviousness can undo that damage at large scales. Many investigations document the local effectiveness of all of the practices we recommend. But at larger scales, research is lacking. The few studies to date do support the beneficial impact of mitigation measures, but they are not yet in the peer-reviewed literature. The lack of research to date is probably a function of the newness of the approach. There are almost no watersheds where mitigation measures have been applied in adequate number to be expected to show an aggregate effect at the watershed scale. Since, as Carl Sagan said, "absence of evidence is not evidence of absence," and the causal link between imperviousness and environmental damage is well established, it seems reasonable to recommend mitigation measures even before their value at larger scales has been authoritatively documented.

Recommendation

Design water handling on-site so that hydrologic conditions are as good as or better than if there were only 10 percent impervious cover and conventional development was practiced.

Developer Benefits

- Lower costs associated with less paving and periodic repaving.

- Reduced maintenance costs.

- Longer life, lower total cost (capital plus operating) for pervious pavement and green roofs than impervious equivalents (Wong et al. 2003).

- Ability to develop sites upstream from sensitive aquatic systems.

- Savings on water conveyance infrastructure because of reduced volume and velocity of stormwater.

- Reduced need for costly treatment to restore water quality because infiltration through soils removes pollutants.

- Easier achievement of NPDES Stormwater Phase II and TMDL permits.

Ecosystem Benefits

- Protects aquatic biodiversity by improving water quality, reducing damaging stormflows, supplementing baseflows, and avoiding habitat destruction.

- Improves water quality by filtering stormwater through soils and vegetation.

- Reduces watercourse erosion, sediment suspension, and loss of aquatic habitat.

- Maintains mix of coarse and soft bottom habitats and low-velocity pools.

- Reduces volume and velocity of stormflow, decreasing the likelihood of combined sewer overflows that threaten public health.

- Avoids artificially low baseflow.

- Reduces damaging stormflows.

- Prevents elevated stream temperatures caused by stormwater heated by sunlit impervious surfaces. High temperatures stress fish directly and lower essential dissolved oxygen in surface waters.

Strategies

- In rural locations that are not adjacent to urban areas, limit impervious surfaces (buildings, parking lots, roads, paths) to no more than 10 percent of total area: **10 points.**

Narrow streets reduce impervious cover while slowing traffic, as cars must share the road with those going in the opposite direction. *Balmori Associates. Adapted from Portland (Oregon) Office of Transportation, 1994.*

28' Roadway (One Parking Lane)

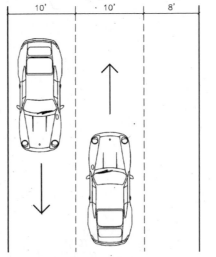

10'   · 10'   8'

Moving lanes   Parking lane

20' Roadway (One Queuing Lane)

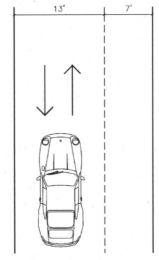

13'   7'

Moving lanes   Queuing lane

NOTE: In suburban locations and in the urban fringe, limiting imperviousness by using larger lot sizes or similar measures promotes sprawl (Jones et al. 2005). In these locations, no points are awarded for limiting impervious area by diluting it with open space. Instead, the several measures listed here should be used because they reduce effective imperviousness while maintaining development density, a desirable goal in urbanized areas.

We use the U.S. Census Bureau's definition of urban. In built-up areas, this is 50,000 people and a population density of at least 600 people per square mile. Outside cities, it is a population center of at least 2,500 people.

- Limit residential street widths to 22 feet (7 meters) rather than the conventional range of 32 to 40 feet (10 to 12 meters): **6 points.**

- Optimize street network to limit its length and area: **6 points.**

- Avoid cul-de-sacs, which increase street length (preferred), or design cul-de-sacs with smaller diameters 33 to 45 feet (10 to 14 meters) or center vegetated islands: **3 points.**

- Place parking spaces below buildings, not in separate garages: **8 points.**

- Provide smaller parking spaces for compact vehicles and carpools. Compact car space size is 8 feet by 16 feet: **4 points.**

- Limit parking spaces: **7 points.**

  Residences: 2 per housing unit

  Motels, hotels, inns: 1 per bedroom

  Retail: 3 per 1,000 feet^2

  Professional/medical: 3 per 1,000 feet^2

  Restaurants, entertainment: 1 per 4 seats

- Use pervious paving materials for all low-traffic areas, especially parking lots and driveways: **9 points.**

- Leave 15 percent of parking areas as rain gardens/bioretention areas. Direct parking lot runoff to these features: **7 points.**

  Studies show that 10 to 20 percent of a parking lot is adequate to handle infiltration (Dussaillant et al. 2004).

Tucking garages underneath reduces the footprint of the building, maximizing green space and eliminating unnecessary impervious surfaces. *David Baker and Partners Architects.*

Water runs or bounces off conventional paving. Porous paving allows water to pass through into the ground while maintaining a hard surface. *Balmori Associates.*

This parking lot at the University of North Carolina at Chapel Hill was constructed using both standard asphalt (left) and porous asphalt (right). Note the water pooled on the left. *Cahill Associates, Inc.*

- Isolate impervious areas to disconnected patches: *5 points.*

- Install green roof systems on buildings: *10 points.*

  Green roofs should be designed to have hydrologic function similar to vegetated areas, to reduce effective impervious area and provide some water quality protection. Green roofs appear to provide intermediate

Standard asphalt   Porous asphalt

The pathways at the Gray Towers National Historic Landmark, Milford, Pennsylvania, are constructed of porous asphalt and incorporate a brick edging for aesthetics. Underneath the paths is an infiltration bed. *Cahill Associates, Inc.*

quality water, between that of a conventional roof and natural vegetated areas (Berndtsson et al. 2006).

- Direct runoff from impervious surfaces to vegetated open areas, or to undisturbed sand and scrub in arid regions: [*5 points* (awarded under Water Conservation and Reuse)].

- Store runoff and use during dry periods: [*10 points* (awarded under Water Conservation and Reuse).]

The green roof on the Ballard Public Library in Seattle, Washington, provides insulation and reduces storm runoff. *Courtesy of American Hydrotech, Inc.*

The many layers of Hydrotech's Garden Roof capture stormwater, while remaining light enough to be installed on almost any roof. *Courtesy of American Hydrotech, Inc.*

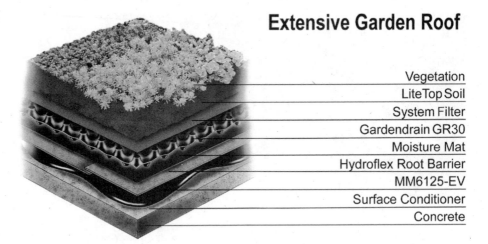

Extensive Garden Roof

Vegetation
LiteTop Soil
System Filter
Gardendrain GR30
Moisture Mat
Hydroflex Root Barrier
MM6125-EV
Surface Conditioner
Concrete

Workers install the largest green roof in New York City at Silvercup Studios. *Joseph Maida, 2005.*

This green roof in San Francisco has both function and high design. *Photo: Jerry Harpur. Design: Andrea Cochran.*

A green roof functions in the same way as a park for stormwater management, heat reduction, air purification, and recreation. *Balmori Associates.*

The bamboo garden on the roof of New York's Solaire Building cleans the air of pollutants and absorbs solar heat, keeping the building cool. *Balmori Associates.*

Plots of vegetation break up an impervious surface area, providing a pathway for water infiltration. *Photo by Catherine Byun.*

Provide tank or pond storage for a 24-hour storm with a five-year recurrence interval. Water can be used for on-site nonpotable purposes, such as irrigation, toilet flushing, and so on (preferred), or can be slowly released to municipal stormwater infrastructure. Runoff released should be of equivalent volume and velocity from that of a site with a maximum of 10 percent impervious cover.

- Use cluster development, placing buildings in close proximity to each other while leaving large, common open spaces: [**10 points** (under Living Resources]).

- Place development near public transit: [**4 points** (under Energy)].

- Limit soil compaction during construction: [**4 points** (under Soils)].
  Soil compacting activities (such as heavy equipment moving, grading, roadways, etc.) can be limited to the immediate construction area. Areas

Clustered housing limits the amount of impervious cover and maintains large, connected green areas. *Photo by Jay Wilson.*

that will not be constructed can be protected with fencing, plan delineations, and signage. Postconstruction tilling can be used as a supplement to preventative practices.

STORMWATER QUALITY

Changes in the amount and timing of runoff are not the only water-related impacts of land development. Precipitation also becomes contaminated as it passes through developed sites. The poor chemical, physical, and bacterial quality of stormwater has been documented in hundreds of scientific studies. Furthermore, the level of contamination is significant, frequently high enough to cause mortality or other substantial harm to a broad array of downstream aquatic organisms (Paul and Meyer 2001).

Watersheds dominated by forests or other undisturbed land cover are generally free from potential contaminant sources. Furthermore, undisturbed ecosystems act to retain or degrade any contaminants that might be introduced. The sources of contamination in developed landscapes may not be obvious on first reflection. Research shows that contributors can include substances leached from building materials (Chang et al. 2004; Rice et al. 2002), chemicals used to treat lawns (Amweg et al. 2006; Groffman et al. 2004), improper disposal of household hazardous waste (Brown 1987), materials issuing from cars and other vehicles (Councell et al. 2004; Sutherland et al. 2001), construction sites (Dougherty et al. 2006; Faucette et al. 2005), septic tanks (Castro et al. 2003; Wernick et al. 1998), wildlife and pet waste (Burnes 2003; Geldreich 1996), drainage from industrial facilities (Line et al. 1996), and deposition from the atmosphere (Shirasuna et al. 2006). (In built-up areas, contaminants may be deposited from the atmosphere in greater abundance, and they are readily washed off paved surfaces.)

These several sources add a witch's brew of contaminants to runoff (Makepeace et al. 1995). Among them are heavy metals (Prestes et al. 2006), pathogenic microorganisms (Petersen et al. 2005), nutrients (Carpenter et al. 1998; Line et al. 2002b), sediment (Coulter et al. 2004), road salt (Jackson and Jobbagy 2005), pesticides (Schiff and Sutula 2004), polycyclic aromatic hydrocarbons (PAHs) (Christensen et al. 1997; Shinya et al. 2000), mutagens (Ohe et al. 2004), and hydrocarbons (Bomboi and

Pouring household hazardous waste into drains or on the ground can pollute the environment and pose a threat to human health. *Photo by Catherine Byun.*

Hernandez 1991). The amounts added are high, both in relation to regulatory limits (Center for Watershed Protection 2003) and compared to levels known to harm aquatic life (Paul and Meyer 2001). For several contaminants, it has been shown that the total amounts of contaminants carried by polluted runoff are greater than those in sewage generated from similar land areas (Laws 1993; Taebi and Droste 2004).

Many strategies for protecting water quality are based on preserving or emulating natural processes. Water that percolates through soils is filtered and loses almost its entire load of suspended sediment and bacteria. Many dissolved contaminants (especially metals and pesticides) are efficiently absorbed by soil particles, and some are biodegraded by soil microorganisms. Plants use nutrients, reducing their concentration in solution. For all these reasons, strategies such as minimizing imperviousness, reducing runoff, and promoting infiltration are just as valuable for protecting water quality as for minimizing the physical impacts of storm flows. Because of these dual benefits, these measures receive points for their effect on both drainage and water quality.

Although many of the same strategies work to reduce excess runoff and protect water quality, some important differences exist as well. For one, infiltration of stormwater has no negative impacts on-site drainage, but it does pose some risk of contaminating groundwater. Likewise, evapotranspiration has the desirable effect of reducing water volume, but it concentrates contaminants in the remaining solution. These concerns should be carefully considered, but, generally, the rewards of promoting infiltration and evapotranspiration outweigh the disadvantages.

Contaminants can be categorized physically as one of three kinds, and different treatment options should be applied to each. Larger particles (> 1 micrometer, includes most pathogens) can be removed by settling in still water. For these, a settling basin, detention basin, or free surface constructed wetland is most effective. Fine particles (< 1 micrometer) do not settle rapidly and must be filtered out. Infiltration basins, sand filters, and subsurface flow constructed wetlands are effective in removing small particles. Dissolved substances cannot be removed by settling or physical filtration, and so must be eliminated by absorption or biological removal. Bioretention areas and subsurface flow constructed wetlands both have been shown to remove a variety of dissolved contaminants. When combining treatment strategies, it is best to remove substances in the order from largest to smallest, as large particles can clog fine filtration media. Thus, for example, a retention basin should be placed upstream from an infiltration basin or subsurface constructed wetland.

In this biofiltration system in Vancouver, a forebay captures runoff from a nearby highway. After the sediment settles out, the polluted water flows into a fully contained biofiltration pond with an impermeable layer, sand, and a growing medium with wetland plants to filter out pollutants. The purified water then flows over the pond into a natural lagoon. *Photo: John Grindon, Brinkman & Associates Ltd. www.brinkmanrestoration.ca.*

There is not an exact correspondence in time between the peak in flow during a storm and the maximum in contaminant concentrations. Instead, for many contaminants, there is an initial maximum in concentration, which occurs before flow has risen to its highest level. This phenomenon, called the *first flush,* can be used to advantage in getting the greatest stormwater quality treatment for the least cost. In many instances, the first flush is not only earlier, but also shorter (sometimes only an hour or so) than the stormwater peak (which typically lasts a day or longer). By preferentially isolating and treating the first flush, it is possible to have the maximum benefit in water quality for the minimum amount of water treated. The trick is to identify which portion of the storm hydrograph includes the first flush. This can be accomplished by modeling, measurement of several storms, or continuous real-time monitoring, which is easily done with fairly inexpensive modern instrumentation.

Besides the low-impact approaches, there are a number of more high-tech methods that can be used to reduce contaminants in stormwater, though they tend to be more costly and require greater maintenance. These include innovative catch basin designs and treatment inserts, advanced in-ground treatment devices, and systems to polish septic system effluent. Compensating for their greater cost and maintenance, they often occupy a smaller footprint than do LID measures, so they are better suited for intensively developed sites.

Modeling water quality is not as easy as modeling water flow. The range of factors that influence the transport and fate of chemicals is greater than the underlying physical processes that govern water movement. Indeed, water movement itself is just one of the elements that need to be known before contaminant behavior can be predicted. For large development projects, models such as the EPA's Hydrologic Simulation Program-Fortran (HSPF) and Better Assessment Science Integrating Point and Nonpoint Sources (BASINS) or the USDA's Soil and Water Assessment Tool (SWAT) can be used to predict water quality. But these models require a level of expertise and knowledge of the characteristics of the site that are usually unavailable in small to medium projects. They also are best implemented at a spatial scale much larger than that of individual development projects. Simpler models exist (e.g., EUTROphication MODel or EUTROMOD, supported by the North American Lake Management Society (NALMS)). These models are based on lumped parameters and empirical relationships rather than spatially distributed data and mechanistic understanding of how systems function. However, they tend to be less flexible and to be limited to specific contaminants and watershed types.

Recommendation

Stormwater leaving a site should be at least as clean as the receiving water into which it flows. Ideally, the water should be as clean as it was before the site was developed. These goals can be accomplished by treating the water on the site, across the landscape, with the same methods described to control peak storm flows, reduce the impacts of imperviousness, and minimize erosion. In addition, measures can be taken that have unique water quality benefits or that apply in circumstances where the intensity of site development obviates extensive use of landscape treatment elements.

In designing treatment measures, the pollutants of highest concern are: pathogens (fecal coliform bacteria, cryptosporidium, giardia, and enterococcus), nutrients (nitrogen and phosphorous), heavy metals (lead, cadmium, mercury, etc.), hydrocarbons (motor oil, gasoline, etc.), pesticides and other organic contaminants, and sediments. This last contaminant category is considered in detail in Chapter 3, in the section titled "Erosion Prevention and Control."

Developer Benefits

- Water quality protection facilitates successful permitting through NPDES and other programs.

- High-quality stormwater may allow development upstream of sensitive ecosystems or in water supply watersheds.

- Development projects that protect water quality are likely to engender less community resistance.

- Lower bacterial levels allow contact recreational use of lakes and streams.

Ecosystem Benefits

- Lower nutrient levels prevent cultural eutrophication, algal blooms, and fish kills downstream.

- Lower sediment levels carry reduced amounts of toxic substances.

- Reduced toxics protect vulnerable communities of aquatic organisms.

- Clear water allows normal light penetration for submerged plants.

- Diminished sediment loads protect filter feeders and bottom dwellers.

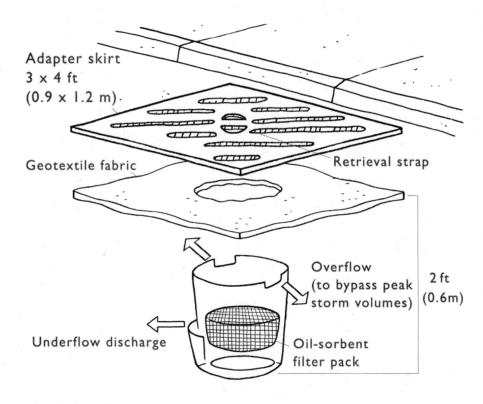

Adapter skirt
3 x 4 ft
(0.9 x 1.2 m)

Geotextile fabric

Retrieval strap

Overflow
(to bypass peak
storm volumes)

2 ft
(0.6m)

Underflow discharge

Oil-sorbent
filter pack

Catch Basin Insert

A catch basin insert filters stormwater through a geotextile fabric and an oil-absorbing filter before it enters the storm sewers. *Daniel R. Abdo. Adapted from Center for Sustainable Design, Mississippi State University.*

To be effective, catch basins must be cleaned regularly with a vacuum. *United Storm Water, Inc., Industry, California*

- Stormwater cooled by infiltration maintains dissolved oxygen levels and prevents stress to aquatic life.

Strategies

- Provide advanced treatment inserts for all catch basins: **4 points.**

- Muck out catch basins whenever sumps become 50 percent full: **4 points.**

- Use mulching mowers and leave grass clippings as fertilizer, or compost leaves and other yard waste and use as fertilizer on-site: **3 points.**

- Use alternatives to halite (NaCl) for road salting: **2 points.**

  Use of $CaCl_2$ avoids negative environmental and health effects of sodium (Ramakrishna and Viraraghavan 2005). Calcium-magnesium acetate (CMA) can be used where there is no risk that biochemical oxygen demand (BOD) caused by acetate will deplete oxygen (Brenner and Horner 1992), for example, where direct discharge to receiving water is avoided.

- Provide dog waste bag dispensers and signage: **2 points.**

  Dog waste is known to be a source of bacteria in urban stormwater (Ahmed et al. 2005).

- Service septic tanks at least every two years: **3 points.**

- Provide polishing of septic tank/leach field effluent: **4 points.**

  Polishing can be in the form of a sand filter, treatment wall, improved microbial treatment, aerobic enhancement, or the like. Down-the-drain additives for septic systems are ineffective and sometimes damaging, and should not be used.

Kitchen scraps and shredded paper produce rich, organic compost that replaces chemical fertilizers. © *2004 Andrew Balinksky/ Balinsky.com.*

Mulching mowers cut grass into fine pieces that fall to soil surface and decompose easily, reducing the need for fertilizer. © 1998 Victa Lawncare Pty Ltd.

- Use constructed wetlands to improve runoff water quality: **7 *points.***

- On heavily developed sites where storage of five-year storms is required, treat any water that is not reused on-site for irrigation or other non-potable purposes: **4 *points.***

- In addition to the strategies already listed, most of those designed to control site drainage, reduce imperviousness, and minimize erosion provide

Road salt can run off into waterbodies, harming or killing vegetation and wildlife. If road salt enters drinking water supplies, it can affect taste, corrode pipes, and contaminate wells. *George Lisensky, Beloit College.*

Sand Filter
(Single-Pass)

Secondary Treatment from Sand Filter and Soil

Removes:
Pathogens
Suspended Solids
Biochemical Oxygen Demand

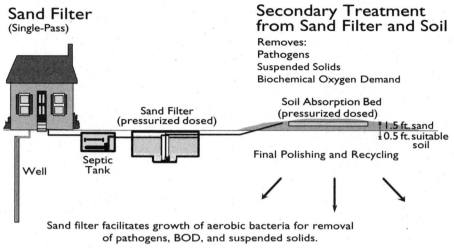

Sand filter facilitates growth of aerobic bacteria for removal of pathogens, BOD, and suspended solids.

Further treatment is achieved in the soil absorption bed.

Controlled amounts of effluent from the septic tank enter the sand filter to be treated by bacteria before entering a soil bed for polishing. *State of Wisconsin, Department of Commerce, Division of Safety and Buildings.*

Constructed Wetlands

Secondary Treatment from Wetland and Soil

Removes:
Pathogens
Suspended solids
Biochemical oxygen demand

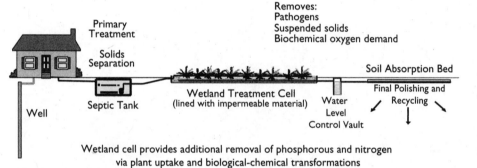

Wetland cell provides additional removal of phosphorous and nitrogen via plant uptake and biological-chemical transformations

The plants in a constructed wetlands process septic effluent by slowing water, to allow sediments to settle, and uptaking nutrients through their roots. *State of Wisconsin Department of Commerce, Division of Safety and Buildings.*

Aerobic Treatment Units (ATU)

Secondary Treatment from ATU and Soil

Removes:
Pathogens
Suspended solids
Biochemical oxygen demand

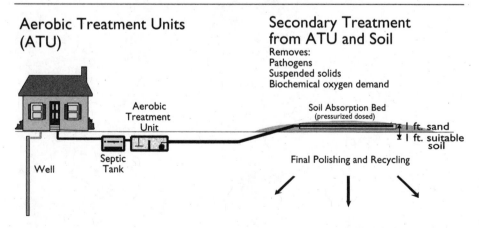

ATU facilitates growth of aerobic bacteria for removal of pathogens, BOD, and suspended solids. Further treatment is achieved in the soil absorption bed.

An aerobic treatment unit supplies a constant flow of air and a stirring mechanism to create an oxygen-rich environment ideal for bacteria to break down organic waste. *State of Wisconsin Department of Commerce, Division of Safety and Buildings.*

Solids settle out of wastewater in the septic tank (forming a sludge layer), while fats and grease float to the top (scum layer). An effluent filter captures small particles in the remaining effluent before it enters the drainfield to prevent plugging of soil pores and extend the life of the septic system. *Daniel R. Abdo. Adapted from National Environmental Services Center at West Virginia University.*

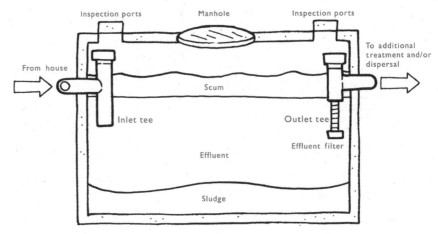

Septic Tank Effluent Filter

The AX20 residential tank is composed of: (1) monitor, (2) processing tank, (3) pump, (4) filter, and (5) recirculating valve. The AdvanTex system works like a recirculating sand filter, but uses a highly engineered textile instead of sand. *Illustration courtesy of Orenco Systems, Inc.*

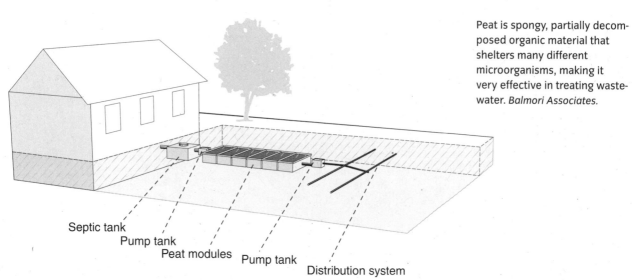

Peat is spongy, partially decomposed organic material that shelters many different microorganisms, making it very effective in treating wastewater. *Balmori Associates.*

Septic tank

Pump tank

Peat modules   Pump tank

Distribution system

Prototypical Residential System

PEAT MODULE SEPTIC SYSTEM

Rain gardens capture runoff from impermeable buildings and pavement to allow for groundwater recharge and water purification. *William F. Hunt III, North Carolina State University.*

A surface flow constructed wetland moves effluent above the soil in a planted wetland. Subsurface flow wetlands move effluent through the soil or gravel in which plants are rooted. They require less land than surface flow wetlands. *Balmori Associates.*

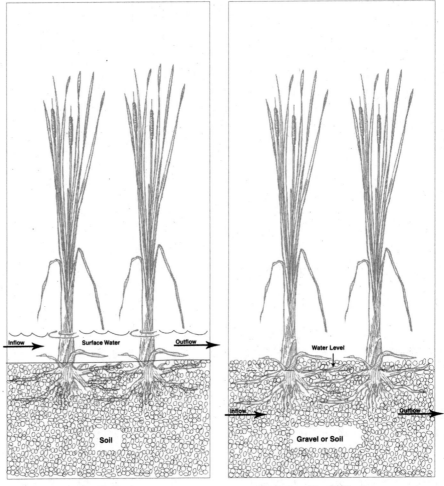

Surface Flow Wetland   Subsurface Flow Wetland

water quality benefits. Credits for the pollution reduction advantages of these measures are included as points in these other sections. Methods include:

- Constructing swales, rain gardens, infiltration basins, detention ponds, green roofs.
- Preserving site contour.
- Immediately stabilizing channels with vegetation.
- Providing 100-foot (30-meter) vegetated buffers for watercourses.

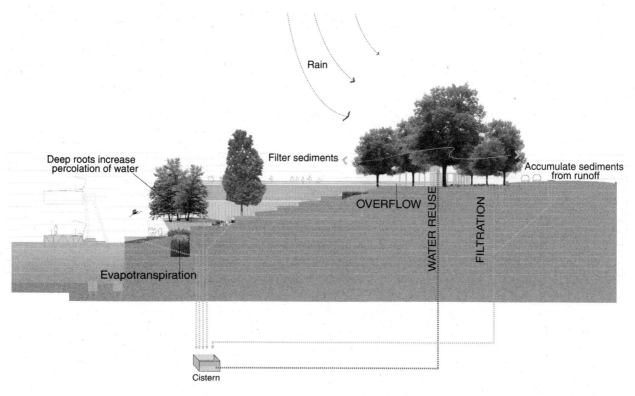

Rain

Deep roots increase
percolation of water

Filter sediments

Accumulate sediments
from runoff

OVERFLOW

WATER REUSE

FILTRATION

Evapotranspiration

Cistern

An underground cistern collects water that has filtered through the soil. The water is reused for irrigation. *Balmori Associates.*

This cistern catches rainwater funneled from the roof and stores it for watering the landscaping. *City of Chicago, Mark Farina.*

- ◦ Implementing various measures that reduce effective imperviousness.

- ◦ Using integrated pest management to minimize pesticide use.

WATER CONSERVATION AND REUSE

Water is a scarce resource. In the United States, water use amounts to fully one-third of the precipitation not lost to evapotranspiration. Conserving runoff on developed sites allows it to be reused for landscape irrigation, to create surface water features, or even to be used for nonpotable purposes indoors, such as toilet flushing. Water thus saved can help reduce utility bills. Demonstration of water conservation and reuse also can send a powerful message of environmental responsibility and stewardship.

Recommendation

Conserve and reuse as much water on-site as possible. Produce creative, visible designs that eliminate the need to use imported, potable water for nonpotable purposes, such as toilet flushing and landscape irrigation.

Household graywater can be captured and cleaned for reuse in irrigation.
www.greywater.com

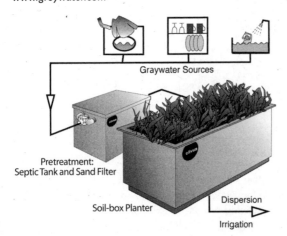

Graywater Sources

Pretreatment:
Septic Tank and Sand Filter

Soil-box Planter

Dispersion

Irrigation

Developer Benefits

- Saves money on utility bills, lowering operating costs of site.

  - Reduces domestic, commercial, and industrial consumption of treated, potable water.

  - Creates pleasing aesthetic experience for users of sites incorporating these designs.

  - Raises public awareness of the importance of water resources, and the ways public and private decisions affect freshwater abundance and quality.

Ecosystem Benefits

- Reduces withdrawals from water supply reservoirs or groundwater for maintenance of healthy aquatic environments and human recreational uses.

- Supplements baseflow in streams.

- Saves energy by avoiding the need to use potable water unnecessarily.

Strategies

- For intensively developed urban sites with inadequate space for bioengineered solutions, capture all the stormwater volume for up to a 24-hour storm with a five-year recurrence interval and reuse it for irrigation: **10 points.**

    A storm with a five-year recurrence interval typically delivers only about 25 percent more water than a two-year storm, so additional costs to store this larger quantity of water are marginal. When water needs of site vegetation are less than captured water, it can be used for other purposes, or released at a rate that will not exceed baseflow levels from an equivalent undeveloped site.

- Use climate-appropriate native, drought-tolerant, noninvasive vegetation for landscaping: **4 points.**

Native wildflowers require no more water than what falls as rain. *Photo by Diana Balmori.*

The moss garden at the Bloedel Reserve in Bainbridge Island, Washington, takes advantage of the mild, moist climate of Puget Sound, which naturally supports a lush carpet of green moss. *Rich Haag, Landscape Architect.*

In dry climates, xeriscapes provide aesthetic landscaping with drought-tolerant plants that do not require irrigation. *Photo by Diana Balmori.*

Use plants that do not require more water than can be provided by local rainfall, supplemented by irrigation water captured from impervious surfaces and stored. This practice is sometimes called *xeriscaping*, especially in arid climates.

- Collect rainwater from impervious surfaces and direct it through landscaped and garden areas needing irrigation: **5 points.**

The stones on this lawn help water to infiltrate the soil while maximizing evaportion during storms and mimimizing it afterwards, reducing erosion, and controlling weed growth. *Photo by Gabe Benoit.*

chapter 3

Soils

EROSION PREVENTION AND CONTROL

Erosion is a serious problem caused by land development. Suspended sediment can block light to submerged aquatic vegetation, clog filter-feeding organisms, bury bottom-dwelling communities, significantly alter aquatic habitat, and carry a major proportion of heavy metals and toxic organic contaminants. Soil erosion is considered the major contributor to nonpoint source pollution (NSP) in the United States, according to the U.S. Environmental Protection Agency (EPA). Contrary to expectations, urban land use causes greater sediment pollution than agricultural land use (Coulter et al. 2004), and up to 10 or 20 times as much sediment can be lost per acre from construction sites as from agricultural fields (Faucette et al. 2005; Line et al. 2002a). Sites that are disturbed for construction activity have soil erosion rates up to 40,000 times greater than the same areas before construction (Harbor 1999). The vast majority of sediment load carried by streams occurs during storms (Dougherty et al. 2006), and sediment export is greatest for construction sites during the rough grading phase (Line et al. 2002a).

As with other aspects of protecting the environment during land development, planning is critical. Several factors influence how much erosion will occur, especially vegetation type and extent, soil characteristics, topography, and weather variables (Science and Education Administration 1978). Erosion can be reduced by limiting clearing of vegetation; avoiding areas with vulnerable soils; staying away from steep, long slopes; and phasing construction to work around local weather patterns (growing season and wet periods). All of these considerations should go into the erosion and sediment control plan.

Plant roots help hold down soil. When cleared of vegetation, steep slopes erode quickly and severely if no effort is made to stabilize the soil. *Sabah Forestry Department.*

Many of the same measures that help to control site drainage and improve stormwater quality are effective in preventing erosion and loss of sediment off-site: grass swales, check dams, constructed wetlands, rain gardens, and infiltration basins. However, an important distinction is that most erosion occurs during the construction phase, so that time period needs to be particularly targeted. A variety of structural and procedural approaches (best management practices, or BMPs) have been devised that are tailored to reducing erosion and controlling sediment during construction. These include strawbale barriers, silt fences, settling basins, and various covers for disturbed soil. There is surprisingly little scientific evidence on the efficacy of these measures, and much anecdotal and observational support that they frequently work poorly or fail completely. The scarce scientific data also suggest that construction-phase BMPs are either intrinsically inadequate (Barrett et al. 1998) or are applied ineffectually (Harbor 1999; Kaufman 2000).

Although existing regulations mandate erosion control during construction, the lack of success of standard operating procedures within the current regulatory framework (Kaufman et al. 2002) argues for new methods. We recommend an approach based heavily on avoiding soil disturbance (in both time and space), using redundant BMPs, carefully monitoring success or failure, and adapting erosion control plans accordingly. For larger projects, there is also a benefit to employing an erosion control contractor independent from the rest of the construction process (Harbor et al. 1995).

Recommendation

Prevent erosion and sediment suspension on-site. Minimize flow leaving the site, to reduce channel erosion downstream. Minimize on-site soil disturbance and stabilize disturbed areas immediately. Divert or otherwise control flow entering the site. Prevent sediment-laden runoff from leaving the site. Use control measures to slow flow, infiltrate stormwater, and remove sediment. Inspect and monitor success, and adapt management strategies as needed.

Developer Benefits

- Conformance with erosion control regulation. NPDES requires a permit for all soil disturbance greater than 1 acre.

- Green (vegetated) sites are perceived by homebuyers and realtors as more valuable than brown (disturbed soil) sites. The increase in value is greater than the costs associated with maintaining vegetation and soil cover (Harbor et al. 1995; Herzog et al. 2000).

- Preventing sediment tracking off-site by vehicles eliminates one of the most common complaints about construction sites.

- Costs associated with periodic sediment removal from water conveyance structures are reduced.

Ecosystem Benefits

- Keeps sediments out of watercourses, maintaining aquatic habitat dependent on gravel substrates and diverse stream channel features, which can become buried with high sediment loading.

- Reduces suspended sediments in surface waters that can block sunlight needed by aquatic plants, choke filter feeders, and bury bottom dwellers.

- Reduces pollutant loading, because heavy metals and other toxic pollutants bind to fine sediment particles and are carried into waterways, where they threaten aquatic life and public health.

Strategies

- Prepare an erosion control map and plan for the site: **Required.**

  The erosion prevention and sediment control plan should map the existing features of the site (topography, drainage, water features, soils, sensitive areas), the proposed grading plan (original and planned final contours, other areas of disturbed soil, stockpile areas for topsoil and subsoil), provide a construction phasing timetable (with due consideration to growing season), and outline the control measures (proposed buffer areas, location of sediment control features, nature of soil protection cover, inspection schedule). The control plan should specify redundancy in erosion control measures and provide alternative strategies that will be implemented should initial measures fail to prevent excessive erosion.

- Clear and grade only those areas that will be included in the construction area: **12 points.**

  Minimizing disturbed soil is critical to controlling erosion. Only the building footprint and a minimal construction envelope should be cleared. This area includes the footprint of buildings, roads, driveways, and parking areas. The envelope should extend no farther than 33 feet (10 meters) from the building perimeter and no more than 6 feet (5 meters) from other features. Areas to be protected should be fenced off and marked with signs.

- Phase construction to minimize simultaneous soil disturbance: **9 points.**

  Erosion losses from a site are proportional to the amount of disturbed soil. Phasing construction at different times for different parts of a site decreases the effective area of disturbed soil. New disturbance can begin once a previously disturbed area is permanently stabilized with vegetation. Soil stabilization with covering material is acceptable as long as it is continuously monitored and renewed until the time that vegetation is established.

- In accordance with the erosion control plan, reduce erosion and manage drainage through the site by installing appropriate erosion control systems prior to clearing land: **8 points.**

Erosion control measures may include soil stabilization with mats, mulch, sod, or hydroseed. Runoff control includes landforms that slow water flow across the land surface, such as properly installed reinforced silt fences and hay bale barriers, check dams on small drainageways, settling basins, earthen dikes, and compost berms. These are more effective the smaller the area from which they receive drainage. Runoff can also be directed to vegetated areas or infiltration basins. Finally, runoff should be stopped at the perimeter of the site and treated, to prevent significant loss of sediment. Depending on the nature of the sediment, this might be accomplished by a settling basin, infiltration, or other means.

Silt fences and hay bale barriers are nearly universally used, but seem especially prone to being improperly employed, or ineffective even when correctly installed (Harbor 1999). Both devices need to be anchored by entrenching the foot below the ground's surface, and hay bales require great care to avoid gaps that spoil their effectiveness. Both systems are effective almost exclusively against sheet flow and should be installed rarely in drainageways. Their function seems to be almost entirely as temporary dams, since their ability to filter water is very limited (Barrett et al. 1998). Recent innovations, including compost and wood waste (either as mulch or berms), show considerable promise (Demars et al. 2004; Faucette et al. 2005; Tyler 2001); some traditional techniques, such as straw mulch, have proven more effective than newer techniques such as hydroseed and polyacrylamide (PAM) (Soupir et al. 2004). Clearly, there is a great need for further scientific research and expert guidance to direct erosion control and prevention (Harbor 1999; Kaufman 2000).

The relative inefficiency of erosion and runoff control measures means that redundancy should be built into the erosion control program. It is also critical that measures be put into place before land disturbance begins.

- Avoid clearing land with slopes between 7 and 17 percent; or, if such slopes must be cleared, stabilize soils immediately with mats, blankets, mulch, vegetation, sod, or the like: *5 points.*

    Erosion is strongly influenced by the steepness of the land, and the rate increases more rapidly than the angle of the slope (Science and Education Administration 1978). The relationship between slope and erosion rate is continuous and has no natural inflection points (abrupt increases). Nevertheless, the entire distribution can be closely represented by three

This silt fence is not functioning properly to hold sediment on one side of the fence. *M. D. Smolen, Oklahoma State University.*

Silt fences control sediment by capturing soil particles from stormwater runoff. *F. Edwards, University of Arkansas.*

straight-line segments covering the ranges from 0 to 7 percent, 7 to 17 percent, and greater than 17 percent slope. This association is the basis for our selection of three slope classes, and the categories are similar to the recommendations of other experts (Prince George's County Maryland Department of Environmental Resources 1999).

There appears to be significant benefit that derives when soil stabilization is applied rapidly and frequently to all bare areas on a construction site (Harbor et al. 1995), and this is recommended but not required for areas with slopes less than 7 percent.

- Do not clear slopes over 17 percent: *5 points.*

Erosion (per area of disturbed soil) increases with the length of the slope, but in a complex way (Science and Education Administration 1978). A steep slope (17 percent) of 66 feet (20 meters) in length is similar to a moderate slope (12 percent) of 200 feet (60 meters) in length or a gradual slope (7 percent) of 1,000 feet (300 meters) in length. Moderate slopes of

200 feet (60 meters) and above should be treated as equivalent to steep slopes.

Leave at least a 50-foot (15-meter) construction buffer along streams, waterways, and wetlands: *5 points.*

The 50-foot (15-meter) buffer applies only during construction. Afterward, a 100-foot (30-meter buffer) is needed (see Chapter 5, "Living Resources"). If construction must occur within 50 feet (15 meters) of a waterway—for example, at a stream crossing—employ engineering techniques to avoid bank erosion and to prevent sediments from entering the waterbody.

- Schedule construction to take advantage of good growing conditions: *4 points.*

  Schedule soil disturbance so that vegetation can be rapidly reestablished during optimal weather conditions.

- Monitor drainage for turbidity throughout construction activities, especially during storms. If benchmarks are not achieved, adjust erosion control practices accordingly, bringing new measures on-line: *Required.*

  Turbidity (cloudiness) of water leaving the site should not exceed 100 NTU, or 10 times the value in the receiving water, whichever is less.

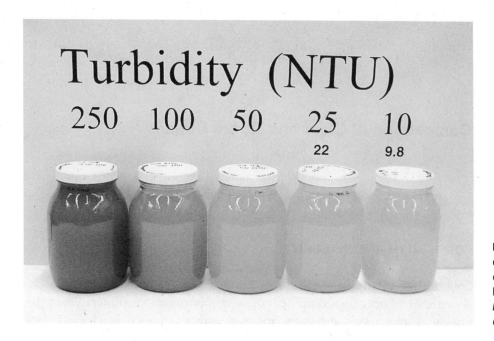

Fine particles of solid matter do not settle out of water, clouding the water. Units of turbidity are measured in NTU. *Photo by NC Division of Water Quality.*

High turbidity blocks sunlight from entering the water and creates excessive sedimentation on the bottom, killing plants and destroying animal habitat. *Balmori Associates. Adapted from Minnesota Pollution Control Agency graphic.*

Clear water with good light penetration
• Lots of macrophytes
• Clean and clear bottom

Murky water with poor light penetration
• Few macrophytes
• Sediment on bottom

Comparison of Clear and Turbid Stream

(NTU stands for *nephelometric turbidity unit,* the standard unit when measuring water cloudiness with a light scattering instrument.)

SOIL HEALTH AND INTEGRITY

Soils are the earth's skin and, as such, are essential components of healthy ecosystems. They are composed of a combination of mineral material, organic matter, water, and gases, and they harbor countless species of plants, animals, and microorganisms. Soils are complex, and each of the 12 major orders has a unique composition and layered structure (called *horizons*). Protecting soils is critical to maintaining multiple ecosystem functions, from plant growth to water purification.

Probably the greatest threat to soils, besides erosion, is compaction. The intricate and delicate structure of soils can be irreversibly altered when it is crushed under the weight of construction vehicles. It can take decades or even centuries to generate healthy new soil once an existing layer has been removed or destroyed.

Recommendation

Preserve soil health and integrity in all parts of the site that are free from buildings and paved surfaces.

Developer Benefits

- Replacing stockpiled topsoil is cheaper than buying new.

- Stockpiled soils contain a seed bank of native plants that are well suited to the local climate.

Ecosystem Benefits

- Healthy soils help regulate the hydrologic cycle, minimize sediment loss, cleanse water, and nurture native plants.

Strategies

- In areas that will be disturbed and later revegetated, remove and stockpile topsoil and replace after construction: *6 points.*

- Avoid compacting soils to maintain soil structure and hydraulic conductivity: *6 points* (points awarded only if low-impact construction methods are used in addition to limiting the construction area; see the section titled "Erosion Prevention and Control" on page 45).

- Aerate compacted soils by tilling and/or other means to restore structure and hydraulic conductivity: *5 points.*

chapter 4

Air Quality and Microclimate

Land development can have a significant influence on air quality and micro-climate. In this chapter, we cover the topics of fugitive dust, beneficial uses of trees, and vegetation that produces air pollution precursors. Dust contributes to respirable fine particulate matter (PM2.5 and PM10), which is linked to a number of diseases (Brunekreef and Forsberg 2005; Delfino et al. 2005). (PM2.5 refers to particulate matter smaller than 2.5 micrometers, whereas PM10 is the name for particles smaller than 10 micrometers. Both are small enough to be carried into the lungs when breathing.) In some locations, construction sites are the major source of atmospheric dust (Chow et al. 1999).

Many plants give off volatile organic compounds (VOCs) that, in an urban setting, can combine with anthropogenic substances under the influence of sunlight to produce smog. It is believed that vegetation accounts for half of the emission of VOCs, which are smog precursors in the United States (Guenther 1997). Plants can have beneficial air quality effects as well, lowering levels of several air pollutants (Nowak 1994). Also associated with land development are air quality impacts resulting directly from buildings, a topic not covered by the LAND Code. Additional important indirect air quality effects are associated with travel to and from sites, as well as the embedded energy of materials. These issues are discussed in Chapter 6, "Energy," and Chapter 7, "Industrial Ecology and Materials," respectively.

Microclimate variables, and particularly local air temperature, humidity, and wind speed and direction, are strongly influenced by land development. Trees alter microclimate by providing shade, lowering temperature, and blocking harsh winds. They also afford numerous other benefits, as they muffle noise, sequester carbon, provide habitat, produce oxygen, stabilize soils, improve the view, and increase property values. Numerous studies have documented the beneficial effect that trees have on microclimate, either at the scale of individual properties (Robitu et al. 2006) or within neighborhoods. For example, one study found that a small park (0.6 square kilometers) lowered the air temperature 1.5 degrees Celsius in a busy commercial area 1 kilometer downwind. This can lead to a significant decrease in air conditioning energy in the commercial area (Ca et al. 1998). Trees have even been linked to lower crime rates (Kuo and Sullivan 2001). For maximum environmental benefits, trees should be considered in terms of their numbers, size, kind, and placement, as described under "Strategies" later in this chapter.

The *heat island effect* is the name given to the higher air temperatures normally found in urbanized areas. Its main cause is enhanced absorption of solar radiation by dark materials routinely used in buildings and pavement. Trees reflect more light back into the sky, directly shade the ground, and consume heat energy in the process of converting liquid water to water vapor (transpiration). Using light-colored paving and roofing materials is another strategy, besides retaining and planting trees, to minimize the heat island effect.

Strategic placement and alignment of buildings on development sites may optimize dispersion of air pollutants (Vardoulakis et al. 2003). However, the effect is complicated (Xia and Leung 2001) and often out of the control of individual developers, so no simple recommendation can be made at present.

Recommendation

Retain as many healthy mature trees on the site as possible. (A mature tree is defined as one that has attained the capacity to flower and reproduce and that has reached 50 percent of its maximum height.) Minimize fugitive dust caused by construction. Determine direction and seasonality of prevailing winds. Plant new trees to block wind and shade buildings.

Developer Benefits

- Trees can be used to block views of neighbors, permitting higher development density.

- Trees provide shade for buildings, people, and parking lots (Simpson 2002) and can save energy (McPherson 1994).

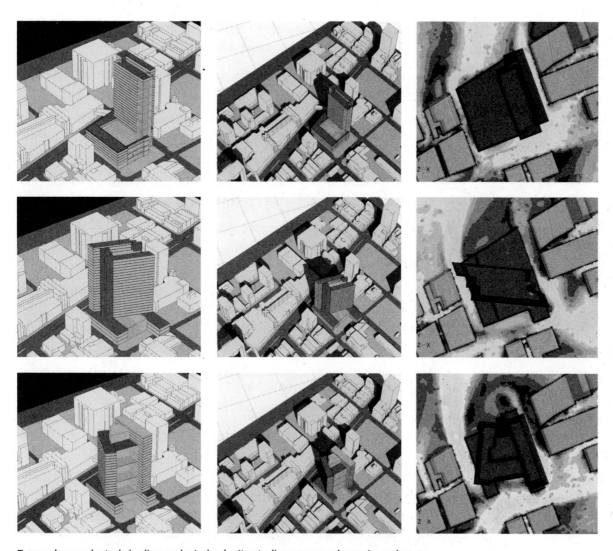

Transsolar conducted shading and wind velocity studies on several massing schemes.
Scheme C was chosen because it performed the best in three areas. Its reduced height minimizes ground-level wind velocity, as well as shading of the plaza to the north. In Winnipeg,
heating energy is of primary importance, both in terms of fresh air heating and heat loss
through the building envelope. The large south-facing atrium of Scheme C maximizes passive
solar heating. © 2006 Manitoba Hydro.

- Vegetation keeps sites cooler in the summer by reflecting sunlight and using heat energy for evapotranspiration.

- Reducing dust minimizes a major source of neighbors' complaints about construction.

- Sites with mature trees have higher property values than those without (Dombrow et al. 2000; Stamps 1997).

- Appropriately placed trees can screen parts of the site from undesirable wind and absorb noise (Fang and Ling 2003; Van Renterghem and Botteldooren 2002), such as that caused by traffic.

- Trees improve a site's appearance (Smardon 1988).

Ecosystem Benefits

- Through the process of photosynthesis, trees produce oxygen and take up carbon dioxide (Nowak and Crane 2002), which contributes to global warming. They can also reduce some air pollutants, including ozone (Nowak et al. 2000) and particulate matter (Beckett et al. 2000).

- Tree roots stabilize soil, protecting it from erosion, especially on streambanks and steep slopes.

- Healthy plants are an important part of both above- and belowground ecosystems. Plants provide shelter and food for wildlife.

Strategies

- Prepare a dust control plan: ***Required.***

  Dust control is aided by many of the same measures used to minimize and control erosion. It becomes more important in arid climates.

- Inventory the mature trees on the site before construction. Identify the number of each species and their sizes: ***5 points.***

  Even a novice can easily identify tree species. Tree size is traditionally measured in terms of a tree's diameter, chest high (diameter breast high, or DBH).

- Retain all mature trees except those on the building footprint and minimal construction envelope: ***10 points.***

  To avoid accidental damage to trees and other vegetation, communicate clear expectations about tree preservation to construction

Trees filter out noise, wind, and air pollution. Studies show that sites with mature trees on them have higher property values than those without.
Above: Photo by Catherine Byun.
Below: Photo by Diana Balmori.

Trees improve a site's microclimate by regulating temperatures, filtering air and blocking wind. They also enhance aesthetics. *Photos by Catherine Byun.*

Mature trees retained on-site provide wildlife habitat and allow for habitat continuity. Wildlife species, such as this red-tailed hawk (*Buteo jamaicensis*) found in New York City, need large trees in order to breed and hunt in urban areas. *Arthur Middleton, 2005.*

contractors. Protect trees during construction with fences and signage. The nature and dimensions of the construction envelope are described in Chapter 3, in the section "Erosion Prevention and Control."

- On sites that are initially sparsely vegetated, plant native trees after construction is completed: **7 *points.***

  Use native or noninvasive trees only..

- Plant deciduous tress to the south of buildings to shade them in summer: **2 *points*.**

- Plant native or noninvasive trees in parking lot rain gardens: **7 *points*.**

  Trees in these locations help promote infiltration and evapotranspiration and simultaneously provide shade for cars and potentially heat-absorbing pavement. Use native or noninvasive trees only.

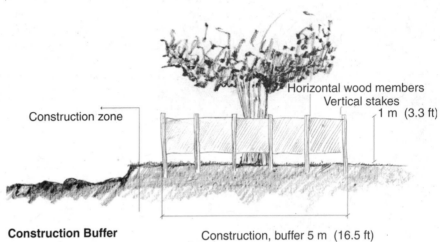

Construction zone

Horizontal wood members
Vertical stakes
1 m (3.3 ft)

Construction Buffer

Construction, buffer 5 m (16.5 ft)

Fences and barriers clearly delineate the construction envelope to protect people and retained vegetation from damage during construction. *Photo by Andrea Mantin. Diagram by Balmori Associates.*

Deciduous trees provide shade for cooling in the summer and allow sunlight to warm the site in the winter. *Photo by Catherine Byun.*

- Wet or rapidly stabilize disturbed soils to prevent dust from leaving the site: *3 points.*

- Determine the direction and intensity of wind on the site: *2 points.*

    Free software and necessary data are available to quickly prepare a wind rose for any location in the United States. One such program is WRPLOT View, available as freeware from Lakes Environmental Software (www.weblakes.com). A novice can run the program in a few minutes.

- Plant evergreens to block the prevailing wind direction in winter: *2 points.*

    Even a single-row, high-density windbreak of trees can reduce energy costs 15 percent (Stathopoulos et al. 1994).

- Leave an open pathway for the summer's prevailing wind direction to provide natural cooling: *2 points.*

    If this requires cutting any trees, replace them by planting elsewhere on the site.

- Use low-emitting plants.

    Many plants produce air pollution precursors, including hydrocarbons and NO_x (Altshuller 1983; Guenther 1997; Penuelas and Llusia 2001; Sillman 1999; Solomon et al. 2000). At present, it is not possible to recommend specific plants because knowledge of which species are acceptable is lacking.

- Where wind energy potential is high, generate electricity with wind turbines: [*6 points* (awarded under Conserving Energy).]

chapter 5

Living Resources

LIVING RESOURCES CONSERVATION PLAN

The loss of biodiversity due to human activities and land-use change has gained worldwide attention in the last decade (Savard et al. 2000). Human disturbances are causing species extinction rates that are estimated to be 100 to 1,000 times as high as historical background rates (Primack 2002b). An analysis of endangered species has shown that the two main threats to species survival are habitat loss and introduction of invasive species (Wilcove et al. 1998). Habitat loss includes outright destruction, as well the negative effects of disrupting population dynamics and fragmenting habitat structure. LAND Code recommendations in this and succeeding sections address ways to mitigate these biodiversity threats during site development. The recommendations are structured to preserve as much habitat as feasible, to set guidelines for mitigating fragmentation effects in the placement of buildings and infrastructure, to promote natural vegetation structures and composition in landscape design, and to encourage active management of the site for biodiversity.

Our advice is based broadly on the recommendations of a committee of the Ecological Society of America on land management. Its report (Dale et al. 2000) outlines ecological principles and guidelines for managing land. Specifically, they recommend that land developers:

(1) examine impacts of local decisions in a regional context, (2) plan for long-term change and unexpected events, (3) preserve rare landscape

elements and associated species, (4) avoid land uses that deplete natural resources, (5) retain large contiguous or connected areas that contain critical habitats, (6) minimize the introduction and spread of nonnative species, (7) avoid or compensate for the effects of development on ecological processes, and (8) implement land-use and management practices that are compatible with the natural potential of the area.

Two of the most important ecological LAND Code recommendations address concerns of habitat loss by encouraging the selection of a previously developed site and by preserving large areas of continuous habitat. Choosing a previously disturbed site reduces development pressures for high-quality habitat areas. Clustering structures within smaller portions of a site and reducing the overall development footprint can preserve considerable site habitat in limited space. Previously developed sites may also contain degraded areas that present the opportunity to create new habitat through restoration. Critical environmental resources, such as wetlands, riparian zones, and areas of rare or endangered species, should be included within preserved habitat areas. Placing buildings and other structures outside buffer zones adds protection to these resources and provides additional quality habitat.

To move away from a patchwork of disconnected landscapes, site design must look at overall landscape patterns and connectivity. Preserving sections of the property that connect to adjacent preserved areas on bordering properties can maintain regional habitat. This is particularly important for animal species that require large territories to find shelter, mates, and food resources. Preserving vegetated corridors for animal migration can promote additional landscape connectivity. Landscaping that does occur on the site should mimic the structure and composition of the surrounding natural environment as much as possible, to provide diverse resources, or niches, that allow for a wide variety of animal life. The choice of native plant species in landscape design is a key component of this principle. Many of the nonnative invasive plants that are problematic today were originally introduced for landscaping purposes (Barton et al. 2004; Brigham 2001).

For conserving living resources, as with other aspects of environmentally sensitive land development, planning is critical. The LAND Code requires a conservation plan for the site's living resources. Its goal is to aid in preserving and restoring habitat, protecting ecologically sensitive areas, buffering critical habitats, promoting landscape connectivity, providing species friendly infrastructure, and conserving native species.

Recommendation

Prepare a conservation management plan that describes the site's living resources and habitat, along with methods to protect them.

Developer Benefits

- Knowledge of a site's unusual living resources allows site development with minimum impact.

- Many special habitats are among the landscape's most beautiful features, so preserving them maximizes a site's economic value.

- Documentation of rare species may be required by the Endangered Species Act or other regulations.

- The plan may comprise a major portion of an environmental assessment, required for some sites by the National Environmental Policy Act (NEPA).

Ecosystem Benefits

- Careful planning helps to preserve a site's plant and animal communities.

- High biodiversity promotes greater ecosystem resilience.

Strategies

- Prepare a living resources conservation plan: ***Required.***
   The plan should include four components: (1) a list of plant and animal species, noting any that are locally rare, threatened, or endangered; (2) a record of the kinds and extent of sensitive areas and special habitats; (3) documentation of the amount and proportion of sensitive areas to be altered by the development; (4) a description of the measures to be taken to protect or restore sensitive areas.

PRESERVING AND RESTORING HABITAT

As described previously, habitat destruction is one of the two greatest causes of loss of biodiversity. A review of the scientific literature reveals that there is no simple threshold for what constitutes an adequate amount of open space or habitat. The answer depends on the particular organism, its life stage, the kind of habitat, the degree of fragmentation or connectedness of the habitat, the type and intensity of nearby land use, the topography, the season, external stresses, predation, food availability, and many other factors. Recommendations exist for individual species (e.g., Wiktander et al. 2001), but these are rare exceptions. In most instances, more open space is better, at least until a very large proportion of the landscape has been preserved. Our recommendation is thus to retain a large proportion of open space and preserved habitat in rural locations that are not subject to sprawl. In suburban areas and the urban fringe, where excessive open space would promote sprawl, the recommendation is for a pattern of development that maximizes pockets of connected open space.

In addition to preserving overall habitat, it is important that the preserved area encompass biodiversity hot spots on the development site. Rare species are part of smaller populations that face higher extinction probabilities. Site design can contribute to maintaining the biodiversity of the region by preserving areas containing rare species and scarce habitat. In addition, rare species are often unevenly distributed geographically (Laurance et al. 2002; McCoy and Mushinsky 1999), and without active identification of their pres-

These detention basins capture and filter runoff from the housing development. *Photo by Bordner Aerials.*

ence and location, vegetation that is cleared for development may eradicate a significant portion of the local population.

Recommendation

Preserve continuous expanses of existing habitat or restore degraded habitat. Protect unusual landforms and sensitive or vulnerable areas. Preferentially redevelop brownfields or other previously disturbed sites.

Developer Benefits

- Open space and varied landscapes are aesthetically pleasing and increase a property's value.

- Greater species diversity protection can be achieved with less land preservation by protecting ecologically rich areas.

- Sensitive areas are often more marginal, expensive to develop, risk-prone, and subject to greater regulation.

Ecosystem Benefits

- Preserving large expanses of continuous habitat on the site supports a larger diversity of species, helps prevent local species extinction, and preserves important interior habitat area.

- Large continuous areas are particularly important for animals that require large territories to find shelter, mates, and food resources.

- Improving habitat quality by revegetating cleared areas and implementing invasive species eradication programs can promote the return of native species and support their successful survival.

Strategies

- Redevelop a brownfield site: *25 points.*

- Redevelop a previously disturbed site other than a brownfield: *12 points.*

- In rural areas not subject to sprawl, maximize preservation of existing habitat on the site as open space.

    ○ Leave greater than 70 percent of site area undisturbed with existing vegetation: *15 points.*

Neighbors on Arch Street in New Haven, Connecticut, worked together and with the Urban Resources Institute to transform three contiguous vacant lots into a lush neighborhood park. *Urban Resources Initiative.*

The AMD&ART project in the coal country of Pennsylvania revived ecologically and culturally devastated lands with an equal balance of the sciences, arts, and humanities. *Before: AMD & ART Project 1994-2005 and T. Allan Comp. After: Holly Lees.*

○ Leave 50 to 70 percent of site area undisturbed with existing vegetation: **10 points.**

- For redeveloped sites in urban areas, restore 20 percent of degraded site to functioning habitat: **10 points.**

  Restoration means bringing back healthy soils, reinstating varied habitat, and exterminating invasives and replacing them with native vegetation.

- In all locations, preserve ecologically, sensitive, physically vulnerable, and unusual landforms and land areas: **10 points.**

  These include steep slopes (greater than 17 percent grade over 100 feet), wetlands, ridgelines, floodplains, vernal pools, shorelines, bluffs, cliffs, caves, riparian zones, ravines, and the like. Also in this category is any habitat that may be uncommon in the area due to past development activities. Examples include old-growth forests and native meadows or prairies.

- Use cluster development to minimize the overall development footprint and concentrate disturbance into one area of the site: **10 points.**

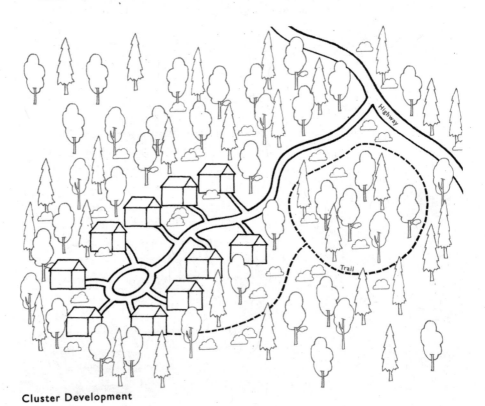

Grouping houses closer together, with easy access to shared outdoor areas, limits overall impervious surfaces and increases green space. *Daniel R. Abdo. Adapted from Pennsylvania Department of Environmental Protection.*

Cluster Development

• Provide a green roof in an urban area: [**7 points** (under Imperviousness)].
  Green roofs can provide some habitat for birds and insects in urban areas. They also offer significant energy-saving, microclimatological, and hydrologic benefits.

BUFFERING CRITICAL HABITAT

The impacts of land development do not stop abruptly at its edge. Many ecosystem variables are altered for distances up to hundreds of feet into adjoining undeveloped lands (Chen et al. 1995; Gehlhausen et al. 2000; Laurance et al. 2002). To ameliorate these impacts, buffers can be placed around ecologically sensitive areas. A buffer is simply a zone of undisturbed land, though it can also be a vegetated strip, intermediate in character, created between a developed site and an undisturbed area.

Buffers slow the flow of water, help capture sediment, and promote infiltration. They also act to remove water contaminants (nutrients, metals, bacteria, and toxic organics). Trees in riparian buffers shade streams, keeping water cooler. Adjacent to open spaces, buffers reduce light, slow winds, afford refuge from predators and severe weather, provide habitat, and act as sources of seeds.

Perhaps most well known are riparian and wetland buffers. To promote pollution abatement, research supports the need for a minimum buffer of 100 feet (30 meters) around these features. Studies have shown that this average buffer width results in approximately 70 percent or greater sediment and pollutant (nitrogen, phosphorous, and total suspended solids) removal (Desbonnet et al. 1995; Fennessy and Cronk 1997). One review suggests that 100 feet (30 meters) is the minimum effective width (Hickey and Doran 2004). Protecting stream hydrology from increased storm runoff, which is critical for stream health, is addressed in Chapter 2. In addition to aquatic ecological health, the riparian zone contains a high diversity of resident species and serves as an important migratory corridor. Additional buffer width above the 100-foot (30-meter) minimum is often needed to preserve targeted species. For example, a buffer of 300 feet (100 meters) has been recommended to support neotropical bird communities (Hodges and Krementz 1996), and a buffer of 500 feet (150 meters) has been recommended for freshwater turtles (Bodie 2001). Amphibians are an example of an especially vulnerable group, because their life cycles contain both an aquatic and terrestrial element. Consequently, they require the conservation of the wetland-upland landscape component. Adult amphibians live in the terrestrial areas but migrate to aquatic environments to breed and lay eggs. Temporary ponds, often referred to as *vernal pools*, as well as permanent small wetlands, are important habitat for amphibians (Dodd and Cade 1998; Preisser et al. 2000; Semlitsch 2000). Preservation of both these habitats and the connection between them are important for amphibian survival. Site development causes physical changes to the environment that can affect amphibian survival capabilities, either directly or indirectly. Roads can create barriers to migration (Demaynadier and Hunter 2000), traffic can cause direct mortality (Carr and Fahrig 2001; Fahrig et al. 1995), and compacted soils or sod can keep amphibians from burrowing into the ground (Jansen et al. 2001). Because of amphibian life histories and the relative rarity of vernal pools, we recommend a larger buffer, of 300 feet (100 meters) for these features, based on the available scientific research (Bulger et al. 2003; Jehle 2000; Joyal et al. 2001; Richter et al. 2001; Semlitsch and Bodie 1998).

Edges allow increased exposure of light and wind into fragmented landscapes. This causes microclimate changes, such as increased temperature variations, decreased humidity, decreased soil moisture, and increased wind turbulence. Overall changes in habitat alter ecological communities by making it easier for invasive nonnative species to take the place of native species (Laurance et al. 2002). Numerous studies have found large physical and community compositional changes within 160 feet (50 meters) of edges (Davies-Colley et al. 2000; Mesquita et al. 1999; Rheault et al. 2003; Young and Mitchell 1994), moderate changes up to 300 feet (100 meters) from edges (Laurance et al. 1998; Laurance et al. 2002), and some alterations reaching 300 to 1,000 feet (100 to 300 meters) from the edge (Chen et al. 1995; Gehlhausen et al. 2000; Laurance et al. 2002). Some edge is normal, even in pristine landscapes, and certain desirable species thrive in such environments. What is problematic is excessive patchiness that leaves little or no deep interior habitat.

Recommendation

Preserve or create buffers to mitigate the effect of human activities on species and to provide additional habitat. Place buffers around important natural resources, such as riparian areas, wetlands, shorelines, vernal pools, and property borders adjacent to nature reserves or parklands. Use buffers to preserve contiguous forest along riparian corridors.

Developer Benefits

- Buffers can increase property values in several ways. For human inhabitants, they improve aesthetics, provide recreational opportunities, muffle noise, and enhance micrometeorology (provide cooling and reducing harsh winds).

Ecosystem Benefits

- Vegetated riparian buffers stabilize riverbanks, prevent erosion, and promote groundwater recharge.

- Streamside trees provide shade, leafy organic matter, and woody debris, which are important components of aquatic stream health.

- Riparian areas provide terrestrial habitat for a rich variety of species, as well as a corridor for migration.

- Buffers around wetland areas are needed to allow soil filtration processes to transform pollutants, to reduce disturbance to wetland species, and to provide habitat for vulnerable species, such as amphibians, that are dependent on the upland border.

- Buffer areas on properties located near public or private natural preserve areas can prevent the introduction of edge effects into the preserve (such as increases in sunlight, wind, and temperature, and reductions in soil moisture).

- Buffers along preserve property borders can stop or reverse habitat degradation associated with edge effects inside the preserves, as well as providing corridors between protected critical habitat areas.

Strategies

- Leave or create an undeveloped buffer of 100 feet (30 meters) around wetlands, streams, lakes, seashores, and adjacent to nature preserves: ***10 points.***

- Create a 160 foot (50-meter) buffer around the same features: ***20 points*** (unless required by local ordinance).

- Leave or create an undeveloped buffer of 300 feet (100 meters) around vernal pools: ***15 points.***
  The larger buffer for vernal pools is appropriate because of the rarity of the habitat type and because of the high biodiversity they contain.

Stormwater slows as it moves through a vegetated buffer, reducing bank erosion. Water infiltrates into the ground, where it can recharge groundwater or be taken up by plants. *Daniel R. Abdo. Adapted from Tom Schultz.*

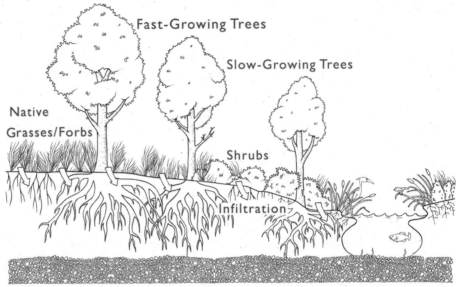

This diagram shows a healthy vegetated buffer in the riparian zone.

Riparian Buffer

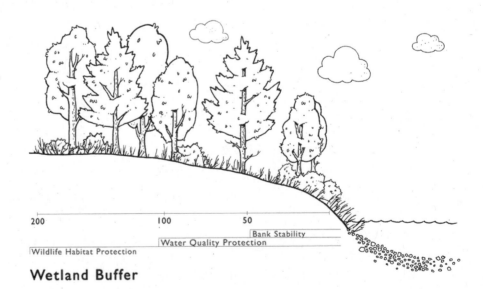

Wetlands are important wildlife habitats that also control flooding and improve water quality. Larger buffers have greater habitat value. *Daniel R. Abdo. Adapted from Vermont Department of Environmental Conservation.*

Wetland Buffer

Lake Shoreline Buffer

Lake shoreline buffers allow soil filtration processes to transform pollutants, and provide habitat for plants and animals. *Daniel R. Abdo. Adapted from University of Wisconsin-Extension and Wisconsin Department of Natural Resources.*

- Design stream crossings by roads to minimize impact: *6 points.*

   Crossing widths should be the minimum needed for function and maintenance, and should be at right angles to reduce the amount of land area disturbed. Only one crossing should be constructed per subdivision or per 1,000 feet (300 meters) for large properties. For small stream crossings, slab, arch, or box culverts should be used, as corrugated metal pipe tends to create fish barriers. The base of the culvert structure should be buried beneath the stream bottom, and a natural bottom surface should be created in the culvert to ensure passage of aquatic life during low flow conditions (Schueler 1995).

   Not all sites may be able to accommodate these buffer requirements, as a result of concentrated urban development or other site design constraints. However, these may be able to employ an alternative buffer design. Specifically, high-density sites ($\geq$ 8 housing units/acre or 24,000 ft^2/acre for nonresidential uses) can use a zoned approach to meet the buffer target of 100 feet (30 meters). The inner 50 feet (15 meters) should be

Vernal pools are ephemeral wetlands that form during wetter seasons. They are critical breeding habitats for many amphibian species. *Photo by Sherry Peruzzi, ©2006. Lower image by Tom Lautzenheiser.*

left naturally vegetated, and use is restricted to stormwater channels and trails (along with necessary utility or roadway crossings). The middle zone should be at least 30 feet (10 meters) and retain natural vegetation, and may include additional limited activities, such as stormwater management and bike paths. The outer zone is the remaining buffer width, and may include common residential backyard activities, with the exception that no septic systems or permanent structures may exist there (modified from Holland 2000).

NOTE: These buffer width recommendations are designed for forested landscapes but are intended to be generally applicable. They do not supersede more specific recommendations for wider buffers that may emerge from the Conservation Management Plan's analysis of the requirements of local flora and fauna.

LANDSCAPE CONNECTIVITY

When landscapes are fragmented by development, maximal environmental benefit can be achieved by linking fragments in continuous corridors (Naiman et al. 1993). Often, these corridors are formed from connecting riparian zones or other linear landscape elements, although other configurations are possible, depending on land availability. Connecting isolated populations across small fragments helps avoid extinction processes. Conversely, fragmentation can compound the effect of habitat loss in causing species decline or loss (Andren 1994). Studies have generally supported the theory that ecological corridors promote movement across the landscape (Debinski and Holt 2000). This is particularly supported for animals that are less mobile and that require specialized interior habitat (Mech and Hallett 2001). The impact of environmental corridors can be significant; the USDA Natural Resources Conservation Service (NRCS) estimates that over 70 percent of all terrestrial wildlife species use riparian corridors.

Continuous, wide, long corridors that include diverse landscape elements are better than fragmented, narrow, short ones that lack variety. Our corridor width recommendations were based in part on Desbonet's literature review (Desbonnet et al. 1995). A study of birds' use of corridors suggested a minimum width of 30 to 80 feet (10 to 25 meters) (Sieving et al. 2000), and a study of mammals by Laurance suggested a minimum of 100 to 130 feet (30 to 40 meters) (Laurance and Laurance 1999). Some state agencies consider primary corridors to have a minimum width of 200 feet (60 meters), while secondary corridors are at least 100 feet (30 meters) wide. Breaks in the corridor are discouraged in general, but site design limitations may require such gaps. A maximum gap distance of no more than 100 feet (30 meters) is allowed in urbanized settings, as breaks greater than this distance have been shown to create a barrier to the movement of many species in continuous forest areas (Laurance et al. 2002).

Recommendation

Take advantage of the many environmental benefits that accrue when patches of undisturbed land are connected in corridors. Promote connectivity and species migration in a fragmented landscape. Leave areas undisturbed that connect to continuous habitat on adjacent properties. Promote species movement through the presence of ecological corridors.

Developer Benefits

- Connected green areas provide a greater sense of open space than disjointed ones.

- Green corridors increase property values (Nicholls and Crompton 2005) even more than open space fragments (Hobden et al. 2004).

- Green corridors can provide recreational opportunities in the form of foot trails and bike paths.

This ecological corridor provides a wide, continuous swath of mixed riparian and forest habitat. *Department of Natural Resource Ecology and Management at Iowa State University.*

Ecosystem Benefits

- Continuous riparian buffers are thought to be one of the most effective ways of protecting species diversity (Moore and Palmer 2005), water quality, and normal flows in urbanizing streams.

- Preserving sections of the property that connect to adjacent preserved areas can maintain regional habitat. This is particularly important for animal species that require large territories in order to find shelter, mates, and food resources.

- Where loss of open space does occur in highly developed areas, ecological corridors help mitigate the effects of the loss.

- Corridors support increased population densities, promote gene flow, and encourage colonization of new areas.

Strategies

Preserve or create ecological corridors that connect habitat areas abutting the development site:

- Preserve a linear corridor with a width of at least 100 feet (30 meters): **_10 points._**

- Preserve or create a linear corridor with a width of at least 160 feet (50 meters): **_20 points._**
    Important corridor parameters are connectivity, width, and continuity (Dramstad et al. 1996). The preserved corridor on the developed site must: (1) connect two patches of undeveloped open space totaling

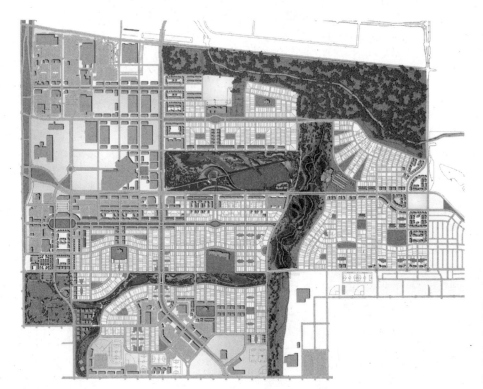

This plan shows how local parks are connected to create large, continuous expanses of open space, which support a greater diversity of species than small, isolated patches.
© 2004 EDAW, Inc.

25 hectares, or (2) be part of a continuous corridor of at least 40 hectares. To be eligible under part (2), the corridor to which the preserved strip on the developed site connects must have no gaps greater than 100 feet (30 meters) long or more than 10 percent of its total length.

ROAD PLACEMENT AND DESIGN

It is estimated that ecosystems on 15 to 20 percent of the land area in the United States are affected by the presence of roads (Forman and Alexander 1998). Roads influence landscape dynamics through direct habitat loss, fragmentation, and an overall decrease in interior habitat. A road placed through a patch of woodland creates edge habitat along part of the perimeter of both new segments. This increase in edge habitat around smaller fragments significantly decreases the interior-to-edge habitat ratio and reduces overall remaining interior habitat. Roads have been shown to inhibit or even block the movement of mammals, turtles, amphibians, and invertebrates, and the wider the road, the greater the problem (Forman and Alexander 1998; Trombulak and Frissell 2000). Road barriers reduce an animal's survival capability by diminishing its ability to forage for food, locate mates and breeding habitat, colonize new areas, and travel during seasonal migrations. The road increases the chances that the overall population will be lost by dividing a previously continuous population into isolated segments. The barrier effects of roads can be mitigated through the construction of passages appropriate to species. Evaluations of animal passages have shown that target species, as well as numerous other local fauna, use these constructed passages (Clevenger et al. 2001; Clevenger and Waltho 2000; Forman and Alexander 1998).

Recommendation

Place infrastructure to minimize habitat loss and fragmentation and to avoid cutting off migration routes. Mitigate a road's effect as a barrier by minimizing road width and by including appropriately designed tunnels, pipes, underpasses, and overpasses.

Developer Benefits

- More abundant and mobile fauna provide opportunities for nature study.

- Lower risk of wildlife collisions with cars can reduce landowner liability (Biggs et al. 2004). Each year in the United States, there are more than 1 million collisions with deer alone. These cause 211 human fatalities, 29,000 injuries, and an average car repair cost of $1,600 (Conover et al. 1995).

Ecosystem Benefits

- Careful placement of a site's access roads can avoid additional landscape fragmentation and the destruction of habitat with high biodiversity value. Roads act as barriers to activities such as foraging, locating breeding habitat, seasonal migration, and colonization of new areas.

- The design and construction of structural measures, such as tunnels, pipes, underpasses, and overpasses can help reconnect separated populations.

Strategies

- Avoid ecologically sensitive areas when building roads: ***Required.***

  Roads have numerous deleterious impacts on living resources. Roads cause mortality during construction and use, modify animal behavior, alter the physical and chemical environment, spread invasive species, and fragment habitat (Trombulak and Frissell 2000). The multiplicity and complexity of these effects, and their substantial variation from site to site, make it difficult or impossible to assign a simple point value. Nevertheless, sustainable land development should seek to direct roads away from locations that contain unique and high-value habitat. These areas, which were identified in the site's Conservation Management Plan, include interior forest habitat, identified rare-species areas, steep slopes, ridgelines, and known animal migratory routes. In addition, in the section "Buffering Critical Habitat" earlier in this chapter, specific points are awarded for buffer zones around wetlands, vernal pools, streams, and shorelines; these zones naturally exclude roads.

Wildlife overpasses—such as this on in Banff National Park, Canada—help mitigate the fragmentation effects of road infrastructure development on wildlife habitat. *Susan Hagood, The Humane Society of the United States.*

- Mitigate the barrier effect of roads by providing road passages, such as tunnels, culverts, underpasses, and overpasses: ***5 points.***

  Use a mix of passage sizes to accommodate a wide variety of species. Amphibians require tunnels from 12 to 40 inches (30 to 100 centimeters) diameter; small mammals use culverts from 1.5 to 3 feet (0.5 to 1 meter) diameter, and medium-size mammals need culverts that are 3 to 5 feet (1 to 1.5 meters) diameter (Clevenger et al. 2001). Entrances to passages should be vegetated with native plants to provide cover from predators. The frequency of passage use is negatively correlated with human disturbances, so place passages away from areas of human activity and direct trails away from the passages (Clevenger and Waltho 2000). Place at least one passage per species home range. For small- and medium-sized mammals, a general minimum guideline would be one passage per 500 feet (150 meters) (Clevenger et al. 2001). Fencing can be used to guide animals to culverts and to prevent animals from crossing roads where high traffic densities are expected.

• Minimize residential road widths to 22 feet (7 meters) rather than the standard 32 to 40 feet (10 to 12 meters): [*5 points* (under Imperviousness).]

NATIVE SPECIES AND LANDSCAPE HETEROGENEITY

Invasive species are one of the two main threats to species survival (Wilcove et al. 1998). Landscaping with native plants is important to support local native fauna populations that have evolved to use local plants for food, shelter, and breeding habitat. Studies have shown that a larger number and variety of native plants support a larger diversity of native birds and insects (McKinney 2002). If exotic landscape plants are chosen, they have the potential to become invasive themselves, or they may transport potential invasive animals, plants, parasites, or disease that attach to the plant during transport (New 2000). Exotics may become invasive if they adapt to the physical conditions of the new area and are not kept in check by predators or disease in the new landscape. Detrimental impacts on native plants include replacing them through competition for resources, herbivory, parasitism, modification of the physical environment, or changes in community dynamics (Henderson et al. 2006; Primack 2002a). Despite extensive research on this topic, the mechanisms that allow invasions are not well understood, nor is it possible to predict invasive traits (Prieur-Richard and Lavorel 2000).

Analysis of rural to urban gradients has shown that the diversity of species decreases and the proportion of nonnative species increases toward an urban center. Much of this is a result of vegetation loss closer to urban centers, but also nonnative plant cultivation within homogenously designed landscapes (McKinney 2002). Instead of reflecting the structural diversity of forested areas surrounding many suburban properties, landscapes are usually designed to approximate "sparsely forested savanna or grassland communities" (McKinney 2002). It is important to include natural variety in landscaping design, as this increases the number of resources, or niches, available to support native species (Carey and Harrington 2001; Ricklefs 1977). It is also important to preserve or create elements such as woody debris piles within the aquatic and forested environment. These piles should not be removed to "clean up" the ground, as they provide valuable shelter, predator protection, and feeding areas for various species (Carey and Harrington 2001; Gurnell et al. 1995). Additionally, standing dead trees, referred to as *snags*, should not be removed from forested areas because they provide similar functions of shelter and protection (Hayward et al. 1993; Lehmkuhl et al. 2006). Studies have shown that preserving or re-creating natural landscape variety may decrease microclimate changes within edge habitat, increase species use of these areas, and promote the migration of species between fragments (Fahrig 2001; Laurance et al. 2002; Ricketts 2001).

Converting lawn into meadow drastically reduces energy-intensive maintenance. *Photo by Catherine Byun.*

Recommendation

Increase habitat value in landscape design by using native plants and promoting naturally wide varieties in structure and composition.

Developer Benefits

- Native vegetation is adapted to local climate, soils, and pests, so it saves money by requiring less irrigation, fertilization, and pesticide use.

- Many native species can be planted at low cost or for free by natural recolonization.

- Structurally varied, biodiverse landscapes appear naturalistic (Lamb and Purcell 1990) and are more aesthetically pleasing (Ozguner and Kendle 2006; Van Den Berg et al. 1998).

- Invasives, unchecked by natural controls (e.g., parasites and herbivores), may spread excessively and require frequent landscape maintenance.

- Natives define the unique local landscape character, providing residents with an enhanced sense of place.

Ecosystem Benefits

- Native plants represent important genetic biodiversity that needs to be preserved, and they are well adapted to survive with limited or no maintenance.

- Native fauna have evolved to use native plants for food, shelter, and breeding habitat.

- Landscape design that includes a variety of local native vegetation, vertical stratification, and appropriate vegetation density creates an environment that provides habitat niches for a wide range of plants and animals.

- Landscapes that are similar to surrounding undisturbed areas promote species migration between habitat fragments.

- Choosing plants with local provenance (geographic source) helps preserve unique local variations in genetic diversity.

- Exotics have the potential to become invasive and outcompete natives, both on the site and elsewhere.

Strategies

- For new landscape plantings select 100 percent native plants, preferably with local provenance: **7 *points.***

  Local provenance in this context means within 250 miles (800 kilometers). Burrell (2001) provides some recommendations for certain ecosystem types. It may be possible to contract with a nursery to grow natives from cuttings. Another option is to collect and store vegetation from the site's development footprint for later reuse.

  Several organizations exist to help landscape designers to identify both native and invasive plants. Many local native plant associations exist and can be identified through contacting local arboretums and searching the Internet. A number of national resources are listed in the reference section at the end of this chapter.

- In undeveloped portions of the site, preserve or create scarce and rich natural habitat elements that are appropriate for the surrounding area: **6 *points.***

  These important environmental elements provide cover and shelter for native fauna. The specific kinds will depend on the local biome, as determined in the Conservation Management Plan. For example, for forested areas, it would include elements such as snags (standing dead trees), windthrows/blowdowns, downed logs, and coarse woody debris.

- Maintain the natural vertical and age structure of the habitat on undeveloped portions of the site: **3 *points.***

  Heterogeneous landscapes provide niches for the greatest variety of plants and animals. A mixed age structure promotes resilience by enabling rapid recolonization after disturbance (e.g., fire or wind damage). Again, the spatial structure is a function of the biome, as described in the Conservation Management Plan. For deciduous forests, it would include the canopy, understory, and ground cover.

- Eradicate invasive species: **7 *points.***

- When pest control must be carried out on the site, use Integrated Pest Management: **6 *points.***

  When pesticides must be used, Integrated Pest Management harnesses state-of-the-art information to minimize human risk and environmental damage (Kogan 1998).

SELECTED RESOURCES FOR IDENTIFYING NATIVE AND INVASIVE SPECIES

Federal Interagency Committee for the Management of Noxious and Exotic Weeds: www.fws.gov/ficmnew. (Note: The book *Invasive Plants, Changing the Landscape of America: Fact Book* is available online at www .denix.osd.mil/denix/Public/ES-Programs/Conservation/Invasive/ contents.html.)

National Invasive Species Council: www.invasivespecies.gov. [Website under reconstruction in 2006.]

National Invasive Species Information Center: www.invasivespeciesinfo .gov.

National Park Service, Alien Plant Invaders of Natural Areas: Fact Sheets, www.nps.gov/plants/alien/fact.htm.

Nature Conservancy, Wildland Invasive Species Program: http://tncweeds .ucdavis.edu.

Wildlife Habitat Council, native plant resources by state: www.wildlifehc .org/managementtools/backyard-stateresources.cfm.

chapter 6

Energy

The United States comprises 5 percent of the world's population, but consumes 26 percent of its energy. Compared to major industrialized countries in Europe, we use twice as much energy per person, with no significant improvement in standard of living. Clearly, there is room for substantial energy savings with little change in quality of life.

Several major environmental impacts result from excessive energy use, especially that derived from fossil fuels. One is generation of carbon dioxide, a greenhouse gas that contributes to global climate change. Another is air pollution from particulate matter, sulfur oxides, heavy metals, nitrogen oxides, and smog precursors. The following recommendations are intended to minimize the overall energy requirements of a site, to reduce fossil fuel use in particular, and to maximize the proportion of energy needs that comes from renewable sources.

The direct energy requirements of most land uses are relatively minor, especially when compared to those of the buildings situated on the land and not considered as part of the LAND Code. The recommendations do not consider energy requirements of individual buildings, or energy use associated with choices of building materials, as LEED guidelines cover both of these topics comprehensively.

The largest energy impact of land development is a consequence of travel to and from a site. Other than site selection, there is little that can be done *at the level of the individual site* to remedy this. For all of these reasons, LAND recommendations relating to energy are relatively few.

Recommendation

Conserve energy and minimize adverse impacts of required energy use. Locate development close to public transportation nodes or provide frequent shuttle service there. Create dedicated preferred parking for carpools and high-mileage vehicles. Provide bike racks and showers. Generate renewable energy on-site. Use only full cutoff light fixtures. Locate buildings to maximize energy efficiency.

Developer Benefits

- Proximity to public transportation increases property value (Armstrong and Rodriguez 2006; Gibbons and Machin 2005; McMillen and McDonald 2004).

- Preventing light pollution by using full cutoff lights allows night skies to be seen more clearly.

- Renewable energy generation can pay itself back in a few years and begin to save money on energy bills.

- Efficient full cutoff light fixtures save money and provide greater security.

- Full cutoff lighting causes less glare, is more beautiful, and attracts business.

- Biking and carpooling reduces the amount of costly parking space that must be provided.

- Residents and employees biking and walking outdoors help to promote interaction and a sense of community.

Ecosystem Benefits

- Generating renewable energy reduces fossil fuel consumption and air pollution, including carbon dioxide production.

- Public transportation is considerably more efficient in terms of CO_2 production per person transported, and in terms of locally produced pollution (Shapiro et al. 2002).

- Locating developments close to public transportation nodes helps prevent sprawl.

United States Annual Average Wind Power

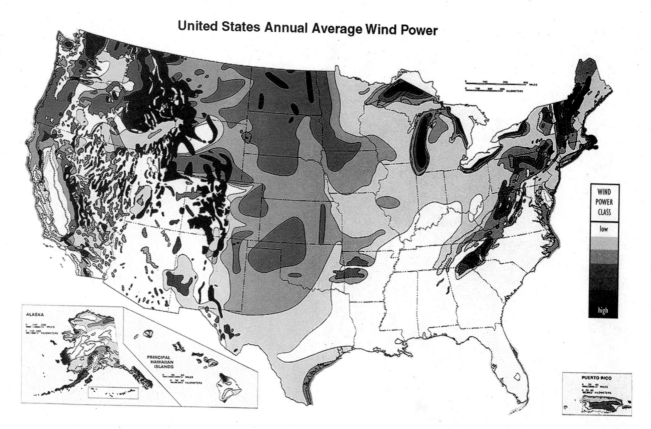

- On-site energy production reduces loss of energy in transmission and, therefore, minimizes waste.

Strategies

- Generate renewable energy with photovoltaics (PVs), wind turbines, microhydropower, or biomass systems: **12 points.**

- Locate site within easy walking distance (1/2 mile, 10 minutes) of public transportation (bus, light rail, or subway station): **6 points.**
  Distance must be truly walkable via a sidewalk or path, not just approximate.

- Choose site within reasonable walking distance (1 mile, 20 minutes) of public transportation: **3 points.**

- Provide frequent shuttle service to mass transit node: **4 points.**

This map of wind energy resources expresses wind power as a seven-class range, from lowest to highest, representing mean wind power for the area. Areas of wind classes 3 and higher are appropriate for wind energy applications. *U.S. Department of Energy.*

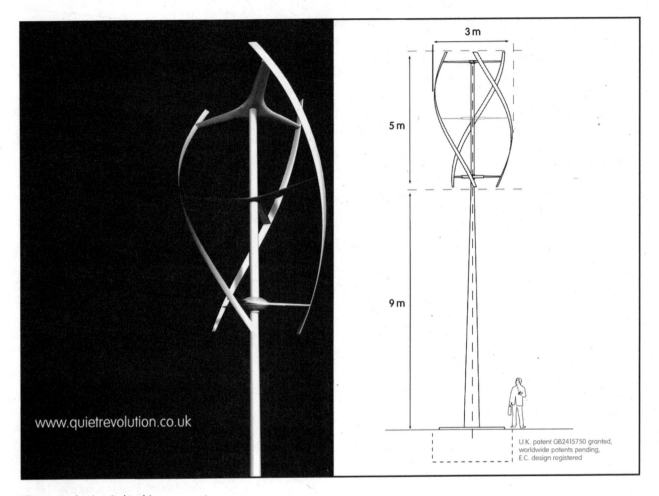

www.quietrevolution.co.uk

3 m

5 m

9 m

U.K. patent GB2415750 granted,
worldwide patents pending,
E.C. design registered

This vertical-axis wind turbine
with a single moving part is virtually silent and vibration-free,
making it suitable for urban
and exposed sites. © 2006
Quiet Revolution Ltd.,
www.quietrevolution.co.uk.

- Provide dedicated preferred parking for high–mileage vehicles and carpools: *4 points.*

   Preferred parking can be in the form of cheaper spaces or ones closer
  to buildings.

- Provide bike racks and showers for muscle-powered commuting: *2 points.*

   For large sites, encourage walking and biking on-site. Create foot/
  bike paths and bike lanes. Include tree-planting strips (curb strips) at
  least 5 feet (1.5 meters) wide alongside sidewalk, and retain or plant trees
  in the curb strip to make walking a more pleasant experience and to
  provide shade in the summer.

Mounted photovoltaic panels at Carkeek Environmental Educational Center in Seattle, Washington, successfully provide a significant portion of the building's energy needs while integrating into a vegetated landscape. *Photos by Robert Dinse, 2005; www.eskimo.com/~nanook.*

Multiple forms of transportation are made possible by providing access to public transportation nodes via alternative transportation means. *John Harvey, 2005; www.JohnHarveyPhoto.com.*

An electric-powered shuttle bus in downtown Santa Barbara, California. *Santa Barbara Metropolitan Transit District.*

Bilbao's 2003 narrow-gauge light rail system allows passengers to use one ticket across multiple transportation types. *Photo by Diana Balmori.*

These photos, taken in Münster, Germany, symbolically visualize the same number of people using different forms of transportation. *From Green Urbanism by Timothy Beatley. © 2000 by Island Press. Reproduced by permission of Island Press.*

By traveling on dedicated road space with priority at traffic lights, this low-floor bus performs like a metro at a fraction of the infrastructure cost. *By kind permission of David Harries, Bristol, England. © July 2005, David Harries; http://buses.fotopic.net*

Dedicated bike paths like this one at Promenade Plantée, Paris, France, create opportunities for efficient, low-impact transportation that does not interfere with pedestrian and automobile traffic. *Javier Gonzalez-Campana.*

Cherry Blossoms on the streets of Lynchburg, Virginia, make walking a pleasant form of transportation. *City of Lynchburg, Virginia.*

Full cutoff lights reduce energy loss and light pollution, thereby protecting the natural night-time environment and reducing harm to nocturnal wildlife and ecosystems. *Adapted from Bill Wren, McDonald Observatory.*

Downward
Streetlight Directionality

Universal

- Use only lights that are full cutoff to reduce energy loss and light pollution: *5 points.*

  The International Dark Sky Association provides information about preserving starry night skies while saving energy on efficient lighting. Its website (www.darksky.org) includes information on kinds and sources of full cutoff light fixtures.

- Plant deciduous tress to the south of buildings to shade them in summer: [*2 points* (awarded under Air Quality and Microclimate)].

- Plant evergreens to block the prevailing wind direction in winter: [*2 points* (awarded under Air Quality and Microclimate)].

chapter 7

Industrial Ecology and Materials

Industrial ecology (IE) is a term that, at first, sounds like an oxymoron—industry and ecology seem like opposites. But IE is simply an effort to emulate elements of sustainability found in nature and to incorporate them into industrial and other built systems, and this can include land development.

Industrial ecology considers the flows of materials and energy through systems created by humans. Some of the elements and tools of industrial ecology are flow assessments, closed-loop recycling, life-cycle assessment, industrial symbiosis, and embodied energy.

- *Flow assessments* analyze the amount and kind of energy and material used to extract, process, transport, and dispose of products and supplies that are used by a project.

- *Closed-loop recycling* seeks to reuse materials after their original purpose is fulfilled, ending the need to dispose of discarded materials in a landfill, where they are wasted.

- *Industrial symbiosis* describes the relationships between industrial facilities if waste from one process serves as raw material for another, often by different manufacturers or industries.

- *Embodied energy* is the idea that all of the energy used to produce an object is embedded in the product, and is lost if it is discarded rather than recycled.

- *Life-cycle assessment* (LCA) evaluates all the environmental impacts associated with a product. These include impacts from generating the materials used in a product, from its manufacturing process, from use of the product during its life, and from the disposal of the product and its constituent parts. LCA includes assessment of the flow of energy and water, and discard streams of air, water, and solid emissions resulting from the product life cycle. The most complete kind of LCA is called *cradle-to-grave* and considers impacts at each stage of a product's life cycle, from the time natural resources are extracted and processed through each subsequent stage of manufacturing, transportation, product use, and, ultimately, disposal.

Applying industrial ecology to land development poses special challenges. For one, much of land development is about alterations to land rather than products in the traditional sense. Many of the life-cycle impacts of site development relate to materials used for buildings, which lie outside the scope of the LAND Code. Also, the lifetime of land development is difficult to predict, or even define. An average building in the United States is used for about 50 years, but what about its site? If a residence is torn down and replaced with another, is that new land use or old? If a factory building is converted into shops or apartments, is that new or recycled? What if a road is repaved or widened? Finally, the lifetime of land development can be so long (a century or longer) that it is difficult to predict the kinds of technologies that will influ-

Industrial symbiosis is the cooperation between companies and municipalities, where one company's by-product becomes a resource to one or many other companies. The result is a drastic reduction of both consumption and waste. *Source: UNEP.*

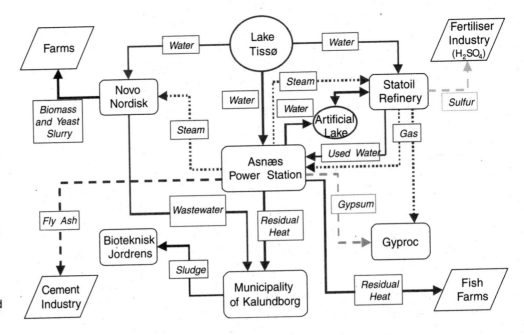

ence it during its existence. As just one example, what will be the major source of energy in 2100, and what will be its cost and environmental impacts?

If a site development lasts for a full century, at some point during that time an industrial ecologist might consider whether it is environmentally preferable to deconstruct a facility that has become outdated and start anew, or to retrofit within the building envelope and retain the embedded energy and materials within the existing structure. Hence, undertaking a life-cycle analysis for a site development incorporates major uncertainties, much more so than undertaking an LCA for a specific commercial product that has a short lifetime, such as a computer or a car.

Within these constraints there remain many opportunities for industrial ecology, recycling, and choice of materials to lessen the environmental impacts of land development. Several suggestions are described in the "Recommendations" section, which follows.

Recommendations

Use as many recycled materials as possible. When you can't recycle, use local sources. Minimize waste.

Developer Benefits

- Less waste means reduced tipping fees and lower costs.

- Using cut material as fill on a site reduces trucking through adjoining neighborhoods.

- Using recycled material can reduce contractor costs for virgin asphalt by up to 80 percent.

- Recycled concrete can be cheaper than virgin aggregate and is suitable for similar applications.

- Recycling certain materials may generate revenue streams for the contractor.

- Using local suppliers and making surplus and recyclable materials available generates goodwill among nearby community.

- Recycled crumb-rubber surfaces improve comfort and safety in pedestrian areas.

- Well-publicized efforts to reduce environmental impacts of a project can generate positive publicity.

- These efforts may also smooth the permitting and approvals process. Many municipal and state governments have formal and informal arrangements for fast-tracking projects that have broad-based community support. New Jersey's Silver and Gold Track Program is an example.

Ecosystem Benefits

- Using recycled material in concrete aggregate reduces waste volume sent to landfills.

- Transportation impacts of removing waste off-site are reduced if concrete and asphalt demolition materials can be reused on site.

- Recycling materials preserves embedded energy and reduces the need for extraction of virgin materials.

- Recycling materials and using local sources reduce the negative air quality and greenhouse gas impacts of transporting construction materials over long distances.

Strategies

- Match cut and fill requirements to eliminate need to import material from off-site: *10 points.*

- To reduce transportation requirements, source 80 percent of all construction materials by weight within 100 miles (330 kilometers) of the site if transported by truck, and within 300 miles (1,000 kilometers) if transported by rail: *4 points.*

  Truck transport emits approximately three times the amount of greenhouse gases as does rail transport, for a given weight and distance of transport.

- Contract with materials suppliers for packaging takeback (e.g., pallets, containers, shrink-wrap, etc.): *3 points.*

  Packaging constitutes a significant proportion of the waste stream in the United States. There is much room to improve the recyclability, or reduce the quantity, of existing packaging. One effective way to reduce packaging overall is to place responsibility with the firms that design and apply packaging to products.

- Make unused materials and recyclable construction waste available to other projects: *3 points.*

    Locate separated reusable materials (e.g., lumber) on-site and publicize materials availability to facilitate possible exchanges. (Many materials exchanges are listed at the end of this chapter.)

- Process and reuse demolition materials on-site, especially concrete and asphalt, *or* source recycled concrete/asphalt from elsewhere: *4 points.*

- Chip removed vegetation for use as mulch on-site: *4 points.*

    Mulching has additional benefits, as described in Chapter 3 in the "Erosion Prevention and Control" section.

- Ensure that only 10 percent by weight of total materials delivered to the site are discarded: *5 points.*

    Methods to achieve this goal include requiring takeback of packaging, careful planning of purchasing, and designing infrastructure to use precut lumber, precast concrete, reusable concrete formwork, and modular components. Furthermore, using prefabricated and/or modular components make disassembly, recovery, and recycling at end-of-life of the project easier and more cost-effective. Construction and demolition waste comprises approximately 40 percent of all material that is sent to landfills in the United States every year. Several studies have shown that diversion rates above 90 percent can be achieved with some basic attention to details, and can even generate cost savings (Begum et al. 2006; Duran et al. 2006).

- Use recycled crumb rubber for paved pedestrian paths: *3 points.*

Additional Resources

BuildingGreen.com (www.buildinggreen.com): This website lists a variety of information on environmentally responsible building construction and design, including a subscription page listing environmentally sound building materials, such as certified wood or postconsumer waste products.

Environmental Literacy Council (www.enviroliteracy.org/article.php/202 .html): The Web site for this organization has links to articles on industrial ecology and a variety of topics, from green roofs, to renewable energy.

Rockefeller University's Program for Human Environment (phe .rockefeller.edu) Here you'll find a variety of articles, under "Publications," that relate to industrial ecology.

Triangle J Council of Governments (www.tjcog.dst.nc.us and www.p2pays.org/ref/11/10172.pdf.): Triangle J has produced guideline specifications to reduce construction waste by building it into the bidding process for use by developers.

Materials Exchange Websites by State (Where Available)

U.S. EPA State-Specific Materials Exchange Information: www.epa.gov/jtr/comm/exchstat.htm

Alaska Materials Exchange: www.greenstarinc.org

California Materials Exchange: www.ciwmb.ca.gov/calmax

Los Angeles County Materials Exchange: ladpw.org/epd/lacomax

NapaMax Materials Exchange: www.napamax.org/Aboutus.asp

Sonomax Materials Exchange: www.recyclenow.org/sonomax

Ventura County Materials Exchange: www.vcmax.org

Colorado Materials Exchange: www-ucsu.colorado.edu/comex

Florida Materials Exchange: www.building99.com/main.php

Southern Waste Information Exchange: wastexchange.org

Georgia Enviroshare: www.hallcounty.org/enviroshare

Hawaii Materials Exchange, Maui Aloha Shares: www.alohashares.org

Illinois Industrial Material Exchange Service: www.epa.state.il.us/land/imes

Indiana Materials Xchange: www.in.gov/idem

Iowa Waste Exchange: www.iwrc.org/exchange/index.cfm

Recycle Iowa: www.iowalifechanging.com/business/recycle.html

Kentucky Industrial Materials Exchange: www.kppc.org/KIME/index.cfm

Maine Materials Exchange: home.gwi.net/~m2x

Maryland Building Materials Reuse Center: www.loadingdock.org

Massachusetts Materials Exchange: www.materialsexchange.org

Michigan Materials Exchange: www.michigan.gov/deq/1,1607,7–135–6132_6828–12382—00.html

Minnesota Materials Exchange: www.mnexchange.org

West Central Minnesota MATCH: www.co.clay.mn.us/Depts/PlanEnvi/SWMATAvl.htm

Montana Materials Exchange: www.montana.edu/mme

Nebraska Materials Exchange: www.knb.org/exchange.html

Nevada Materials Exchange, Washoe County Materials Exchange Network: www.nevadamax.org

New Hampshire Materials Exchange: www.wastecapnh.org/nhme

New York Waste Match: www.wastematch.org

Hudson Valley Materials Exchange: www.hvmaterialsexchange.com

Ohio's Material Exchange: www.epa.state.oh.us/ocapp/p2/omex/omex.html

Hamilton County Interchange: www.hcdoes.org/sw/interchange.htm

South Carolina Waste Exchange: sc.wastexchange.org

Tennessee Materials Exchange: www.cis.utk.edu/TME

Texas Resource Exchange Network for Eliminating Waste (RENEW): www.tceq.state.tx.us/assistance/P2Recycle/renew/renew.html

Vermont Business Materials Exchange: www.vbmex.net/otherexchanges.html

Washington Reusable Building Materials Exchange: www.metrokc.gov/dnrp/swd/exchange/index.asp

Washington, Oregon, and Idaho IMEX: www.govlink.org/hazwaste/business/imex

Northwest Materials Exchange: www.nwmaterialsmart.com/index.html

West Virginia Materials Exchange: www.state.wv.us/swmb/exchange/Index.htm

Wisconsin Business Materials Exchange: www.bmex.org

University of Wisconsin: www.bussvc.wisc.edu/swap

chapter 8

Environmental Engineering

A wide diversity of engineering methods are available to achieve sustainability in land development projects. Some emulate natural systems closely, while others use the same processes in an accelerated or enhanced way. The former are often cheaper, lower maintenance, and lower energy, and frequently provide multiple benefits (e.g., habitat enhancement, hydrologic regulation, and water quality protection). At the same time, approaches that mimic natural systems commonly require a larger footprint than more high-tech methods and sometimes need more time to accomplish the same results. Intensively engineered solutions can often achieve results in a smaller space and more quickly, and are thus better suited to more densely developed locations. The LAND Code is results-based, not technology-based, so one method is not preferred over another.

This chapter describes some of the engineering tools that are available to achieve sustainability. Both green engineering and traditional methods are included. Both benefits and disadvantages are explained, as well as how the system works. In some cases, costs and sources are listed, especially for proprietary systems with one or just a few providers. Note that inclusion in this chapter is not an endorsement; nor is exclusion intended as a criticism. Whatever works on your site is the best method for you.

EROSION PREVENTION AND CONTROL

Preventing and controlling erosion keeps excessive sediment out of waterbodies, protecting soils and habitat and guarding water quality. Many existing, widely used methods seem to be only partially successful at controlling erosion (Kaufman 2000), so multiple levels of protection should be employed. It is especially important to be vigilant, as small breaks in protective measures can have major consequences. Many of the methods described here can work only when applied at or near the source, and this is the preferred strategy. Removing sediment once it has been carried downstream is difficult, and disposal is problematic. Many in-stream measures applied at downstream locations appear to be ineffective (Kochel et al. 2005), and adaptive management (essentially trial-and-error) is recommended in such instances (Johnson et al. 2002). Much better is to keep sediment on the site, where it is a resource, helping to form needed soil. Often, local ordinances require the prevention of sediments running off-site and mandate certain measures be employed. Be sure to monitor and actually prevent erosion, not just fulfill the letter of the law.

Mulches

Mulches (thin layers of organic material) are typically used in combination with seeding on exposed soils to prevent runoff during the initial stage of vegetation establishment. Mulches are effective in preventing sediment runoff because they absorb the rain's impact, which typically suspends solids; they absorb some water; and they help to prevent rill erosion (formation of incipient channels). Mulches should be applied to exposed soil as soon as vegetation is removed, or at least before the first storm (Harbor et al. 1995). A very wide variety of materials have been used as mulches, including hay, wood chips, compost, yard waste, hydroseed (a mixture of seed, mulch, fertilizer, water, and a tackifier to hold the seed in place before it germinates), and polyacrylamide (PAM, a synthetic material). Mulch should be tacked down with a string grid or tackifier, or be mechanically punched into the ground. Recent innovations, such as compost and wood waste (either as mulch or berms), show considerable promise (Demars et al. 2004; Faucette et al. 2005; Tyler 2001), but some traditional techniques, among them straw mulch, have proven more effective than newer techniques, such as hydroseed and PAM (Soupir et al. 2004).

Mulches have the added benefit of helping to suppress and delay runoff of water (Krenitsky et al. 1998). In one study, straw and turfgrass sod were compared to wood excelsior (shavings), jute fabric, coconut fiber blanket, and coconut strand mat. All were effective at preventing erosion, but only sod, straw, and jute also significantly decreased runoff (Krenitsky et al. 1998).

Wood chips, normally a waste product, and easily produced by a chipper from removed vegetation on-site, are effective at reducing erosion from bare soils. A mixture of sizes is best, followed by large chips (Buchanan et al. 2002). Yard waste, another material often discarded, is an effective mulch with a significant capability to prevent rill erosion. Compost also works well (Persyn et al. 2005) and has no negative impacts on water quality (Glanville et al. 2004).

Mats and Blankets

Mats and blanket are used to stabilize exposed soil where seed growth or general erosion control is desired. These differ from mulches in being thicker and often having woven or other structure to them. They can be made of both woven synthetic (e.g., plastic) and natural (e.g., coconut fiber) materials and are useful on steep slopes. Mats and blankets cover the soil, and water should not be allowed to flow freely beneath it. Metal stakes and/or staples can be used to keep mats and blankets in place, and proper installation to ensure this condition is crucial. Recent innovations include a spray-on application made of interwoven fibers (Schueler 2000). Blankets are generally more effective than mulches (Benik et al. 2003).

Silt Fencing and Straw Bales

Silt fencing consists of a geotextile fabric that is staked to the ground at the base of an area of exposed earth. It takes up little space, is easily installed, and is relatively cheap. These factors have made it perhaps the most widely employed erosion control strategy; however, it often fails due to improper maintenance and installation. It is critical that the base of the fence be anchored by burial at least 6 inches into the ground; an unanchored fence has no effect at all. Silt fence and hay bales can only control erosion once it has occurred; they cannot prevent it. Thus, they should be used in conjunction with erosion *prevention* measures such as mulches or blankets.

Studies indicate that silt fence does not act as a filter, but rather as a dam (Barrett et al. 1998), forming a temporary settling basin. This has two important consequences. First, the fence must be supported in a way that allows it to hold back the considerable weight of ponded water, not just captured sediment. Second, any gaps between sections, substantial tears and holes, or spots where the bottom of the fence is not entrenched allow rapid passage of water,

Permanent turf reinforcement mats are a "soft" alternative to concrete or riprap applications for roadside channels. Once vegetation is established, the netting remains. *Photos courtesy of North American Green.*

The photodegradable polypropylene netting and straw and coconut filling of this mat degrade within a year.
Photos courtesy of North American Green.

**Cross Sections of
Trenches for Silt Fences**

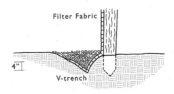

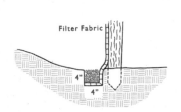

How to install a Silt Fence

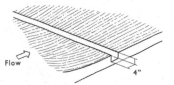

1. Excavate a 4x4 trench along the contour.

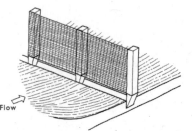

2. Stake the silt fence on downslope side of trench.
Extend 8" fabric into the trench.

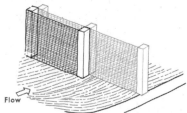

3. When joints are necessary, overlap ends for
the distance between two stakes.

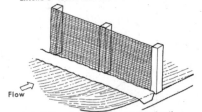

4. Backfill and compact the excavated soil.

Silt Fences

To properly install silt fences, 4-inch trenches must be dug and 8-inches of fabric buried into the soil. *Daniel R. Abdo. Adapted from North Carolina Erosion and Sediment Control Planning and Design Manual, 1988.*

eliminating its effectiveness. One method to strengthen silt fence is to reinforce it with a chain-link fence. Though at this level of construction, building one or more check dams might make more sense.

Straw bales serve the same purpose as silt fence and must be installed just as carefully. Again, they should be entrenched at least 6 inches, a precaution rarely seen in the field. They need to be anchored with stakes or rebar, and gaps between them must be avoided. In practice, this essentially requires a double layer of bales, also something rarely seen in practice.

In numerous installations, silt fences and hay bales appear to be nothing more than Band-Aids or the perfunctory response to erosion control ordinances. Use them properly and as part of a multilevel erosion prevention and control system.

Organic Berms

Low berms formed from compost or wood waste have been shown to be superior to hay bales and silt fence in their capability to capture eroded soil particles (Demars et al. 2004; Tyler 2001). Once seeds grow and stabilize the slope, these materials can be worked into the soil, eliminating the need for disposal.

Fiber Logs

Fiber logs can be installed around the perimeter of exposed soils to prevent sediment runoff. Coir fiber can be used, and is expected to be more durable than a straw blanket. Logs are typically more expensive than silt fences, but are much more attractive. However, they may require more maintenance. Fiber logs also have been tested as a method to prevent shoreline erosion (Sistani and Mays 2001).

Fascines

Fascines are long, rope-like bundles of branches or twigs, generally tied together in some fashion. They can be laid along contours on steep slopes to catch eroded material. They work best when they are partially entrenched or staked in place.

Coir Fiber

Coir fiber stabilizes substrate and provides good conditions for plant growth. Coir is a coconut fiber with high tensile strength, moisture-retentive properties, and a decomposition rate suitable for use as a temporary substrate stabilizer. It is commercially fabricated into bioengineering modules, some of which contain pregrown plants. It can also be used as a mulch or blanket. Coir fiber bioengineering modules may not be suitable for in-stream use where high energy flows can undermine their effectiveness.

- Pregrown plant carpets provide wide coverage for immediate habitat and erosion protection.

- Fiber rolls stabilize banks and permit the establishment of vegetation. The coir fiber accumulates sediment and biodegrades as plant roots develop, stabilizing the soil.

- Coir fiber baffles also have been used to increase the effectiveness of sedimentation ponds (Thaxton et al. 2004).

Coir fiber logs prevent erosion and sediment runoff and degrade over time as plant growth occurs. A proper installation includes stakes to hold the natural fiber log in place. *Charles Mayer.*

This slope showing general instability is treated with 6-meter (about 20-foot) rods to hold the surficial rocks to the more stable underlying quartzite layers. Coconut fiber blankets control erosion and provide a base for revegetation. In three months, the slope is fully revegetated with no erosion gullies. *Deflor Bioengenharia, www.deflor.com.br/.*

In environmentally sensitive areas where synthetic materials may pose a threat to wildlife or habitat, a fully biodegradable bionet, made from jute netting, straw fiber filling, and cotton thread, degrades in one year. The interwoven strands of the top net move independently, reducing the risk of animal entanglement and enabling planting. *Photos courtesy of North American Green.*

Shoreline and Streambank Protection

The following measures apply to shoreline and streambank erosion, where there is significant flow of water. Use of these techniques is somewhat specialized, however, and may be problematic where high flows have significant destructive energy, especially during storms (Johnson et al. 2002; Kochel et al. 2005; Simon and Steinemann 2000).

- *Live stakes*: Live stakes are plants that can stabilize streambanks after rooting. They can be used to anchor other erosion-control devices, such as fascines, log toes, brush mattresses, and erosion-control fabric. Live stakes, which are often inexpensive, are derived from hydrophilic plants whose cuttings have good rooting abilities.

- *Branch boxes*: Branch boxes are used as offshore breakwaters. They can provide 5 to 10 years of shoreline protection before biodegrading. Branch boxes are composed of tied rolls of dead branches anchored parallel to the shoreline by vertical stakes, which also are typically made from wood. Branch boxes should be viewed as temporary measures (several years), hence requiring periodic replacement.

To stop further erosion of this slope after a debris slide, bundles of live willow poles were set into the contours of terraces to hold back eroding material until they sprouted roots that would stabilize the slope. *Pierre Raymond of Terra Erosion Control Ltd.*

In this slope stabilization project in Vancouver, a geotextile blanket and a wattle fence hold the growing medium in place. Live stakes and brush layers revegetate the slope with native plants. *John Grindon, Brinkman & Associates, Ltd.; www.brinkmanrestoration.ca.*

This sandbar willow pole, shown after 1.5 years of growth, is one in two rows of poles that were installed on the slope of a stream stabilization site on the Turtle River, in Grand Forks County, North Dakota. The slope above the willow poles was seeded with native grasses and forbs and native trees and shrubs, and covered with an erosion blanket. *Red River Regional Council's Riparian Project, Grafton, North Dakota.*

- *Other techniques:* A number of other streambank protection measures are described in (Li and Eddleman 2002) and the streambank erosion manual published by the Iowa Department of Natural Resources (2006; available as a PDF download from www.ctre.iastate.edu/erosion). In-stream measures need to be applied cautiously, as stream geomorphology is often controlled by larger-scale watershed properties that cannot be circumvented locally by in-stream measures.

Monitoring Turbidity

Successful reduction of sediment loss during construction of developed sites requires frequent monitoring and readjustment of prevention and control measures. The simplest and quickest way to check success is by measuring

The riverbank was reshaped to a more gentle, stable slope; a brush mattress armored the slope and provided a base in which to plant live willow stakes. A rock toe further protects the channel from the eroding force of the water. *Red River Regional Council's Riparian Project, Grafton, North Dakota.*

water turbidity, or cloudiness, which is a good surrogate for suspended sediment. Typically, one unit of turbidity, or *nephelometric turbidly unit* (NTU), corresponds to about 1 milligram of suspended matter per liter of water. Levels vary by region, but numbers between 1 and 10 NTU are common in many areas. Test a clean local stream to get a baseline value.

Turbidity can be measured by a nonspecialist, either at single points in time or continuously (preferred). It is especially important to test during storm flows, when values tend to be greatest. Turbidity meters are made by Lamotte, Hach, Oakton, and Hanna Instruments, among others. Expect to pay between $500 and $1,000 for a good-quality unit. Continuous measurement is possible by using a Yellow Springs Instruments (YSI) water quality meter data logger system (e.g., model numbers 6820, 6920, or 6600) with the 6136 turbidity probe. The meters cost about $4,000, and the turbidity probe an additional $1,300. These systems also provide data on temperature and dissolved solids at no additional cost or effort, and other water quality characteristics can be added. This is a small investment compared to the cost of many land development projects, especially where the system will be used for many projects.

Sculpted forms are constructed from local riparian material and shaped to conform to the contours of eroded streambanks and gullies. Willow components take root and reinforce the recovery action. *The Watershed: An Ecological Installation, 2001; artist Daniel McCormick, Marin County California. Photography: Pamela Cobb.*

Other Resources

An excellent and thorough guide to preventing and controlling erosion is available from the Kentucky Division of Water (www.water.ky.gov/sw/nps/Publications.htm). Also, the Center for Watershed Protection makes available a wealth of useful information on erosion and other water issues (www.cwp.org/).

STORMWATER MANAGEMENT: RUNOFF QUALITY AND QUANTITY

Stormwater from developed areas produces destructive flow amounts and carries high levels of contaminants. Solutions to both of these problems often involve retaining, infiltrating, and treating runoff near its source. Many measures that reduce runoff volumes also protect water quality, so engineering methods for both are considered together here.

Stormwater runoff carries pollutants that are washed off of impervious surfaces, such as rooftops, parking lots, and roads. In built-up areas, storm flows are often directed into municipal underground storm sewer systems that deliver it to a wastewater treatment facility. During large storms, treatment plants are unable to accommodate heavy volumes, so polluted runoff is rerouted directly to receiving waterbodies without treatment. Pollutants commonly found in stormwater are comparable to raw sewage in amounts of characteristics that include hydrocarbons, sediments, heavy metals, nutrients, temperature, and bacteria. In an effort to prevent these contaminants from entering waterbodies, a number of applications exist that enable on-site treatment and attenuation of stormwater.

Soil Aeration

Soil aeration can be helpful in areas where soil compaction inhibits infiltration. Compaction alters soil structure and hydrology by increasing soil bulk density; breaking down soil aggregates; decreasing soil porosity; and by increasing water runoff and soil erosion (Kozlowski 1999). Designating selected areas where construction equipment can travel and park, covering soil with a thick layer of coarse aggregate rock to absorb weight, or using equipment that is distinguished by its capability to disperse its weight over a large surface area can reduce the need for soil aeration. Previously compacted soils can be aerated by tilling, injection of high-pressure gas (e.g., Terravent), or use of spike or plug aerators, with or without soil amendments (e.g., peat, wood chips, grass clippings, straw, compost, sawdust, or vermiculite) to provide a less dense soil texture. Aerators can be rented or purchased at low cost (around $200 per day).

Plants roots inside three test tubes with increasingly compacted soils illustrate the effect of soil compaction on root growth. *Mahdi Al-Kaisi and Stephanie Nelson.*

Dry Wells

Dry wells are for infiltration of runoff into the subsurface. Their design is usually in the form of an underground gallery filled with coarse gravel to provide a combination of temporary storage capacity and surface area in contact with the aquifer. Advantages of dry wells are minimization of aboveground infrastructure, groundwater recharge, and low aboveground space requirements. One of their

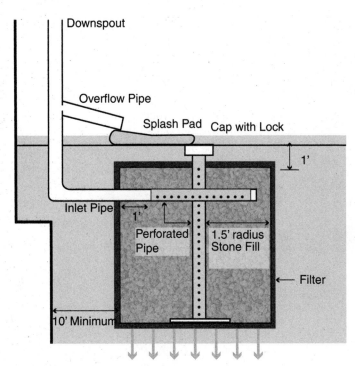

Downspout

Overflow Pipe

Splash Pad   Cap with Lock

1'

Inlet Pipe

1'

Perforated Pipe

1.5' radius Stone Fill

Filter

10' Minimum

Section through Dry Well

A drywell routes stormwater to an underground gravel-filled chamber to help it infiltrate the ground. *Balmori Associates. Adapted from T.R. Schueler.*

disadvantages is the risk of contaminating groundwater. They can be installed only where soils are well drained and the water table is several feet below the surface.

Underground Vault/Tanks

Underground vaults are designed to capture and, sometimes, treat on-site stormwater. They are typically installed beneath parking lots that are graded to drain to the vault, though they can also be used to detain water draining from rooftops or other impervious areas. The vault can be designed so that water undergoes a series of settling and filtration treatments prior to discharge. Advantages include increased water quality and minimal aboveground space requirements, and the ability to be placed in heavily developed locations. Disadvantages include cost and maintenance. ConTech is one company that produces an array of vaults and treatment systems (www .contechstormwater.com/products).

This rainwater harvesting system has a small pump outfitted with a pressure tank, pressure switch, and float switch to effectively and economically distribute the collected water to where it will be used. *Nic Koontz, Clemson University Sustainable Agriculture Program.*

Rainwater Harvesting

Capturing on-site rainwater from impervious surfaces for irrigation or other building needs reduces demand for potable water. Systems are typically designed to capture rooftop runoff and direct it via downspouts to a sand filter that is connected to a storage tank located inside or outside the building (above- or below-ground). The simplest system is a rain barrel located beneath each downspout. Rooftop water quality is generally good (Thomas and Grenne 1993), especially after the roof has been washed by initial rainfall. Wasting the first flush of water is a simple method to avoid much of the contaminant load. The harvested water can be used for irrigation or treated for building use, including toilet flushing and laundry. Use as drinking water is also possible with adequate treatment, pathogens being the greatest health risk (Lye 2002). Treatment technologies exist that are sized to fit in a home or small building. Harvesting reduces the need for municipal infrastructure and water demand. Rainwater harvesting is most useful where water is scarce or its quality is questionable. A detailed

This rainwater harvesting system collects a maximum of 1,500 gallons of water at a time and can meet the irrigation needs of the building and landscape for a three-week drought. This demonstrates the viability of rainwater collection and utilization techniques for small farmers and homeowners. *Nic Koontz, Clemson University Sustainable Agriculture Program.*

guide to rainwater harvesting is available for free download from the Texas Water Development Board website (www.twdb.state.tx.us/publications/ reports/RainwaterHarvestingManual_3rdedition.pdf).

Permeable Paving

Permeable paving can substantially reduce runoff and promote infiltration in parking lots, walkways, and other typically impervious areas. A wide variety of products are available, including porous asphalt and concrete, block pavers, and plastic grid types. The following are some examples of products that may be used in certain applications to replace traditional impermeable paving materials.

- *Porous concrete:* Pervious concrete has an open texture with extensive connected void space that allows infiltration of water. Infiltration rates of 5 inches/minute are commonly achieved, equivalent to the most intensive downpours. A greater limitation can be infiltration below the concrete. Porous concrete should be installed over 6 to 8 inches of coarse gravel to allow temporary storage of the water and percolation downward. One study found infiltration rates were high enough to yield negligible runoff for rainfall events with a 100-year recurrence frequency in South Carolina (Valavala et al. 2006). Installation is by conventional ready-mix trucks; a curing time of seven days is recommended. Thus far, pore clogging has not been a problem, and it can be reversed by vacuuming or pressure washing. Freeze/thaw characteristics allow its use in cold climates, but care should be taken to avoid sanding in winter. It is believed to have a lifetime equal to conventional concrete. Installation cost is slightly greater, but total costs may be lower because of the possibility of eliminating or downsizing drainage infrastructure. There is some evidence that microbes inhabiting the pores of the concrete can remove nutrients (Park and Tia 2004) and hydrocarbons from infiltrating water. The porous texture leaves a somewhat rough surface that may be damaged by heavy traffic (surface raveling). One product is Enviro Concrete from Tarmac America (www.tarmacamerica.com/tarmac/ products/readymix/pervious.html).

- *Porous asphalt:* This material is similar in many ways to porous concrete. Fines are removed by screening from standard asphalt before installation, leaving a porous structure that allows rapid infiltration of water. Installation is over 18 to 36 inches of aggregate for the same purpose (storage and percolation) as the concrete equivalent. A layer of porous geotextile at the bottom allows water through while preventing upward migration of fine soil particles. Many installations have been in place for over 20 years. Cost is similar to conventional asphalt and lower than concrete. Use in cold climates is possible, as there are no freeze/thaw problems; sanding should be avoided. Maintenance can include annual vacuuming, though this is not required. Care must be taken to avoid coating or sealing out of ignorance of the pavement's function. A minor disadvantage associated with any asphalt pavement is leaching of hydrocarbons (Mahler et al. 2005; Pengchai et al. 2004), though reclaimed asphalt has low values (Legret et al. 2005), perhaps because it is previously "weathered."

- *Plastic grid/grass:* A number of manufacturers produce plastic grids (interlocking honeycombs, rings, etc.) that stabilize the surface and allow grass to grow while preventing soil compaction and killing of roots. A substantial portion (50 to 100 percent) of the plastic is recycled, providing additional benefits. Generally, these systems can support the weight of heavy vehicles, though they are not recommended for heavy-traffic areas, but rather parking lots, fire lanes, and the like. These materials come in sheets or rolls and are installed over a layer of gravel and/or sand. The spaces are filled with a soil/sand mix and planted with grass or covered with sod. Established areas require essentially the same maintenance as lawns or athletic fields. According to the manufacturers, maintenance requirements over the life cycle of the product will be lower than those of traditional asphalt pavement. Conventional equipment can be used for snow removal, as long as skid plates are added to keep plow blades above the pavement surface. There is some risk of freeze/thaw damage with some of these products. Finished installation resembles a grassy field. Several manufacturers are listed here.

    Grasspave2: Invisible Structures, Inc., 20100 E. 35th Drive, Aurora, Colorado 80011–8160; 800–233–1510; www.invisiblestructures.com

    Geoblock: GeoCHEM, Inc.; 907–562–5755; www.geocheminc.com

    Grassroad Pavers: NDS, Inc., 851 North Harvard Avenue, P.O. Box 339, Lindsay, California 93247; 800–726–1994; www.ndspro.com

    Grassy Pavers: R.K. Manufacturing, P.O. Box 7300, Jackson, Mississippi 39282; 800–957–5575; www.rkmfg.com

Grass-Cel: Multi-Stream,126 Joo Seng Road, 05–11 Gold Pine Industrial Building, Singapore 368355; 65–288–3020; www .multi-stream.com.sg

- *Porous block pavers:* These are prefabricated concrete blocks with large holes that can be filled with gravel or vegetation. They can also be used to line groundwater recharge basins. Installation typically involves a sub-grade of gravel covered by a permeable geotextile with a sand layer and pavers above. About 40 percent of the surface remains uncovered and is available for planting, compared to up to 90 percent for plastic grids. Total thickness is around 12 inches. Porous concrete pavers are able to withstand loads even greater than those of plastic grids, though load-bearing ability is not a disadvantage of either type. Three manufacturers are listed here.

  Turfstone: Interlock Paving Systems, 802 West Pembroke Avenue, Hampton, Virginia 23669; 757–723–0774; www.interlockonline.com

  Checker Block: Hasting Pavement Company, Inc., 640 Muncy Avenue, Lindenhurst, New York 11757; 301–620–0100; hastingsarchitectural.com/checkerblock.htm

  Grasscrete: Grass Concrete Ltd., Walker House, 22 Bond Street, Wakefield, West Yorkshire WF1 2QP, England; 44 (0) 1924–379443; www.grasscrete.com/index.asp

Vegetated Drainage Channels

Ordinary drainage channels simply convey water from one point to another, usually as quickly as possible, with significant risk of erosion. Vegetated channels can detain water—lowering storm peaks—allow infiltration, and promote some water quality improvement.

- *Grass channels* are less steep than most conventional channels, but are steeper than wet and dry swales. As the name implies, they are completely vegetated. Flows must be low enough to prevent uprooting the vegetation. Design criteria can be found in Schueler (2000).

- *Dry swales* may have standing water during and immediately after storms, but are dry most of the time. They are small linear detention basins. Ideally, they should be constructed to retain the entire volume of the desired design storm (recurrence interval). The lack of water allows them to be mowed if desired.

- *Wet swales* can be created in areas with shallow water tables, and they contain standing water most of the time. They are, effectively, small, elongated, free-surface constructed wetlands. Wet swales should be planted with emergent wetland plants that are able to pump oxygen to their roots, preventing anaerobic conditions that hinder biodegradation of contaminants.

Infiltration Basins

Infiltration basins are larger detention impoundments designed to allow percolation of water to the subsurface. They can be constructed only in areas with well-drained soils. To prevent groundwater contamination, these basins should receive only high-quality runoff or stormwater that has been treated to remove noxious dissolved substances. Water residence times of one to three days are usually required, but longer periods of standing water are undesirable. Infiltration basins remove fine particulate matter by filtration, and larger particulate matter should be eliminated upstream of the basin to prevent clogging. One design is to include a sediment forebay to receive the first flush of polluted runoff containing the majority of coarse suspended matter. Routine maintenance of the forebay is crucial to ensure settling of larger sediments prior to the flow's entrance into the main basin. During construction, it is important to avoid soil compaction, which would limit percolation. Basin success requires high permeability, and dredging of sediments may be necessary, if permeability noticeably decreases. An emergency spillway should be provided to prevent erosion of the basin berm when the basin's design capacity is exceeded.

Blackwater Treatment

Blackwater is the product of toilet flushing and high solids sources, such as garbage disposals. (Most water from washing and bathing qualifies as graywater, which is lower in contaminants and bacteria.) The standard method of disposal is with a septic tank and leach field. The tank allows physical removal of floating and sinking constituents, as well as a limited amount of biological

An infiltration trench is a linear structure similar to a typical subsurface infiltration basin, suitable for areas with limited space. A perforated underground pipe allows water to distribute itself along its length into a stone bed wrapped in geotextile fabric. *Cahill Associates, Inc.*

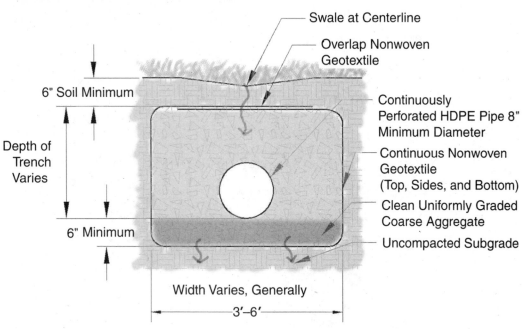

Subsurface septic chamber for secondary or tertiary treatment of blackwater. *John Strutt.*

treatment. The leach field disperses the effluent in gravel-filled trenches, where bacterial films provide further cleansing. Final treatment is via filtration by the soil.

Here we describe a few systems designed either to polish septic system effluent or to replace one or more components in locations with small surface areas or shallow water tables. These devices provide the equivalent of secondary or tertiary treatment for septic systems. Depending on the system, the final polished effluent can be leached into a designated area or recirculated into double-plumbed homes for further blackwater use. Use of a specific system is generally regulated by local ordinances, which should be consulted. Disadvantages can include cost, maintenance, and energy requirements, though these are generally modest, and the treatment systems may permit development of sites that would otherwise be impossible with conventional technologies. What follows are a few well-known systems. The U.S. EPA has detailed descriptions of an extensive list of treatment designs at its Center for Environmental Industry and Technology (CEIT) website (www.epa.gov/region1/assistance/ceit_iti/tech_cos/waswat.html#septic).

(1) The dosing tank holds effluent from the septic tank, pumping it in controlled amounts to the next chamber. (2) Bacteria in the secondary treatment media provide the first round of biological treatment. (3) The recirculation tank receives the effluent and pumps it in controlled amounts to the overhead sprinklers. (4) Spraying the partially treated water adds oxygen, causing hyperactivity in the bacteria. (5) Water that falls on the secondary treatment media is recirculated. Water that falls on the tertiary treatment media (which has never received raw sewage) undergoes a final polish before discharge into a drainfield, waterbody, or quaternary treatment. *SPEC Industries, Inc.*

AIRR SYSTEM
(Alternating Intermittent Recirculating Reactor)

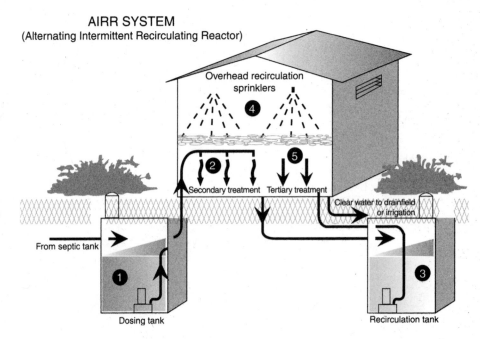

AIRR Wastewater Recovery System (SPEC Industries)

The Alternating Intermittent Recirculating Reactor (AIRR; www
.specind.biz) uses biological activity and oxygenation to treat domestic septic tank effluent. The process involves media filtration
(gravel), a recirculation tank, spray nozzles for oxygenation, and
bacterial hyperactivity upon the surface of the media. Installations
can be designed odor-free to allow leaching under patios or near
buildings. The high quality of the effluent, which is clear in color,
enables it to be disposed to surface waterbodies—with an NPDES
permit—in poorly drained soils. Units can be installed above- or
belowground, and other facilities can be built on top of subsurface
installations.

There are no climatic constraints; the average pump life is over
8 years (some have lasted 20), and media may need to be replaced
or washed on rare occasions. There have been no failures since the
first installation in 1977, and this system can serve single or multiple housing units. Costs range from $6,000 to $10,000.

Orenco AdvanTex Treatment System

The AdvanTex Treatment System is a recirculating packed bed filter that's similar to a recirculating sand filter, but it uses a highly
absorbent engineered textile (instead of sand) for the treatment media. This
enables the patented AdvanTex Filter to treat a high volume of waste in a
small area. The residential AX20 model, for example, has more than 1 acre of
surface area for wastewater treatment in a footprint of only 25 square feet,
while the commercial AX100 model boasts approximately 7 acres of surface
area in a footprint of 122 square feet. The system requires an upstream primary settling basin (i.e., a septic tank) and an area for effluent dispersal downstream. Treated effluent can be used for subsurface irrigation. An ultraviolet
(UV) disinfection device can also be added to the system.

Residential equipment (excluding the tank and drainfield) lists at $5,500.
Installation costs vary greatly depending on terrain and prevailing wages,
but they are at least as much as equipment costs. Similarly, annual maintenance costs vary greatly depending on local regulations, testing requirements, and prevailing wages, but they are typically equivalent to or less
than monthly municipal sewer fees. The system includes a "smart" remote
telemetry control panel that can diagnose problems and troubleshoot solutions. Commercial-sized systems are coupled with an Orenco Effluent Sewer
(www.orenco.com/ots/ots_adv_index.asp) to provide wastewater treatment

The exterior of the AIRR system
can be designed to suit any
style. Only the tank covers in
the ground indicate that the
shed houses a septic polishing
system. *SPEC Industries, Inc.*

for subdivisions and whole communities, with flows ranging from 2,500 to 250,000 gallons per day (gpd).

Equaris Bio-Matter Resequencing Converter

The Equaris Technologies (www.equaris.com or www.waternunc.com/gb/Equaris_Corp01_2002.htm) are distinguished by their capability to separate and compost kitchen organic waste matter and toilet blackwater, in the Bio-Matter Resequencing Converter (BMRC), and biologically treat the remaining graywater in their separate tanks, utilizing extended aeration. The composted matter is safely reusable as fertilizer for nonedible plants and trees. The treated graywater can be safely discharged to a very small drainfield or can be totally recycled into potable water, utilizing the Infinity Water Recycling System, which utilizes ozone, ultrafiltration, and reverse osmosis. The Infinity-treated water is superior to bottled water and is then totally reusable within the home or business (even including drinking), and no wastewater effluent is produced or discharged. With the Infinity system, no well or septic or piped water or sewer is needed. Makeup water is collected via rainwater harvesting from the roof and stored in two 500-gallon cisterns. The systems come with a five-year warranty. Costs including installation range from $17,000 to $40,000.

Clivius Composting Toilet and Graywater System

The Clivius system (www.clivusne.com) splits waste into blackwater and graywater components and treats them separately. It is applicable to new stand-alone applications and existing systems. The standard composter can accommodate three foam flush toilets, and its compost is not recommended as a fertilizer. The system is ordinarily installed in the basement. Capital costs (including installation) are around $11,000, and annual O&M costs (energy, bacterial additives, and inspection) are around $250.

Living Machine

Living Machines (www.livingdesignsgroup.com) are multifaceted systems that can treat both black- and graywater to graywater reuse standards. Treatment occurs in a series of sealed and open tanks mainly within a greenhouse. Treatment steps may include anaerobic and aerobic reactors, clarifiers, constructed wetlands, ultraviolet disinfection, composting reed beds, and filtration, among others. Effluent quality is comparable to conventional secondary treatment (Todd and Josephson 1996).

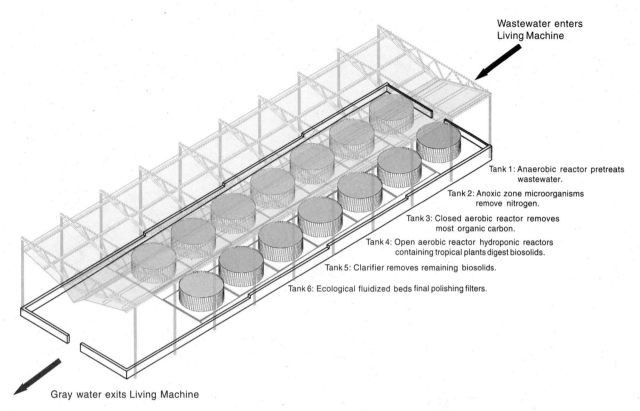

Wastewater enters
Living Machine

Tank 1: Anaerobic reactor pretreats
wastewater.

Tank 2: Anoxic zone microorganisms
remove nitrogen.

Tank 3: Closed aerobic reactor removes
most organic carbon.

Tank 4: Open aerobic reactor hydroponic reactors
containing tropical plants digest biosolids.

Tank 5: Clarifier removes remaining biosolids.

Tank 6: Ecological fluidized beds final polishing filters.

Gray water exits Living Machine

The Living Machine process is distinguished from traditional wastewater treatment by its greater use of plants, larger number of smaller treatment steps, and operation within a greenhouse, factors that greatly improve aesthetics over traditional sewage treatment plants. For that reason, Living Machines can often be built in locations where construction of conventional plants would be resisted. Footprint and energy consumption are similar to those of conventional treatment (Brix 1999).

Living Machine systems are often used when wastewater treatment and demonstration or education are equally important objectives. One advantage of a Living Machine is that people have the ability to flexibly manipulate the various stages of the treatment process to meet changing needs once it is installed. In addition, the volume of sludge produced is lower and may be reused as fertilizer. Systems range in capacity from 2,500 to 100,000 gpd. Living Machines can be purely solar-powered, as demonstrated by an example in Washington, DC.

Living Machine wastewater treatment systems use a series of tanks that mimic water purification processes found in natural systems: an anaerobic septic tank, an anoxic reactor, a closed aerobic tank, an open aerobic reactor (with plants and other organisms), a clarifier, an ecological fluidized bed, often followed by a constructed wetland. *Balmori Associates.*

Living Machines make use of natural bioremediation processes to treat wastewater, including blackwater, and serve to educate the public about bioremediation. *Balmori Associates.*

RENEWABLE ENERGY

A number of methods exist to produce renewable energy on even small sites. Each has its advantages and disadvantages and not all methods are practical or even possible in every location. Benefits range from lessening air pollution to lowering greenhouse gas emissions to reducing dependence on foreign oil.

Photovoltaics

Solar power is probably the most common form of small-scale renewable energy generation. Photovoltaic (PV) panels convert sunlight directly into electricity, which can be used immediately as direct current (DC), stored in batteries, or converted to alternating current (AC), with the option of selling power back on the grid. PV is most practical in areas with low cloud cover and abundant sunshine.

Like all renewable energy strategies, practicality of PV increases with the local cost of electricity that it replaces. Many states offer substantial financial incentives to purchase PV, and financing through home equity loans is another method to get a tax break. The most common location for installation of PV panels is on buildings, and especially roofs, but units can also be set up in any open location. Environmental costs include the embedded energy and resources needed to create the panels, and the trees or other natural features that they displace. Cost for PV panels is likely to decline as use increases, a side benefit that could accrue from many development projects establishing small individual applications.

Building integrated photovoltaic (BIPV) systems have several benefits, including the capability to be used in lieu of traditional roofing materials or wall components, which saves on material cost and waste production. The high visibility of BIPVs provides an opportunity for building developers and occupants to demonstrate a commitment to a sustainable relationship between the built and natural environments. They can also be pleasing features of a building, though some people would resist them on aesthetic grounds.

There are several manufacturers and distributors of PV power systems. A good list, searchable by location, business type (e.g., manufacturers, retail sales businesses, wholesale suppliers, system installation, architectural services, nonprofit organizations, and trade organizations), and name, can be found at the Photovoltaic System Businesses in the World website, http://energy .sourceguides.com/businesses/byP/solar/pvS/pvS.shtml.

Wind Turbines

Wind power is one of the cheapest and most widely applicable forms of renewable energy. Per unit of electricity produced, wind power is generally less than half the cost of PVs. Not all locations are suitable for wind turbines, however, because wind resources are distributed unevenly around the country. The Wind Energy Resource Atlas of the United States includes maps showing where wind energy is greatest (http://rredc.nrel.gov/wind/pubs/ atlas/maps.html). Generally, generating electricity from the wind is practical where the wind power class is 3 or above, somewhat less than half of the area of United States. Many such locations are sensitive areas (e.g., mountainous regions) or remote from most human users. In some other places, zoning regulations prohibit wind turbines. Where it is practical and permitted, wind turbines have a short payback period (typically just six to seven years), so they are worth serious consideration in these locations.

Microhydropower

Locations with flowing water, especially on steep sites, can harness microhydropower. Hydropower is reliable, predictable, and changes little with day/night cycles. Equipment used to convert falling or flowing water energy to electricity is dependable and can work for years with little maintenance. On the downside, there are few locations with suitable water supplies. To be practical in driving an electric turbine, water must descend a distance of at least 6 feet (2 meters) on the site, and greater head is better. Horizontally flowing water can be harnessed for mechanical energy (waterwheels), but such applications are rare. One website that provides a listing of microhydropower businesses is http://energy.sourceguides.com/businesses/byP/solar/pvS/pvS.shtml.

Biogas/Anaerobic Digestors

Organic waste can be converted to methane through simple anaerobic digestion. The technology is extremely simple, requiring nothing more than a reaction vessel that is closed to the atmosphere, and the method is widely used in developing countries. Any biodegradable organic matter can be used, from animal waste to yard clippings. The product gas is nearly a pure mixture of CO_2 and methane, which burns cleanly. The biogas can be used as fuel for heating, cooking, or lighting. A website with information for biogas beginners is www.ees.adelaide.edu.au/pharris/biogas/beginners.html.

COMPUTER MODELS

Designing a development project to be environmentally sustainable requires careful planning. Computer models can be invaluable tools in this process by allowing prediction of outcomes based on selection of design parameters. A number of different possible designs can be tried out and outcomes evaluated with little expenditure of time or money.

Models differ in their complexity, accuracy, data requirements, ease of use, flexibility, generality, and cost. For small development projects, some excellent free models (often supported by government agencies) can be used by novices to produce useful results based on data that is widely available on the Internet or elsewhere. As development projects become larger and more complicated, it is likely that the only adequate models will be very sophisticated and require considerable technical expertise—though the same could be said for virtually all aspects of such projects.

In the lists that follow, we describe some of the many models that are available to help design development projects. Attention is given to the models' features, limitations, ease of use, and availability. More models are available to simulate various environmental aspects of buildings than the land on which they are situated. Some of these models of building systems will be mentioned briefly, though their application is largely indirectly related to the focus of the LAND Code, namely development of the land itself.

Stormwater Flow

Rational Method

- Calculates peak flow for one or more subcatchments based on the formula: $Q = C \times i \times A$, where C is a runoff coefficient, i is the rainfall intensity, and A is the subcatchment area. The runoff coefficient is the fraction of water leaving an area as surface flow. It varies from 0.05 (5 percent) or less for some vegetated surfaces to 0.95 (95 percent) or higher for impervious surfaces.

- Very simple model, suitable for small watersheds.

- An interactive website is available to facilitate calculations (www.geocities .com/Eureka/Concourse/3075/rational.html), although they can be done easily by hand or in a simple spreadsheet.

HydroCAD

- A stormwater modeling system used for the analysis, design, and documentation of complete drainage systems using standard hydrograph techniques.

- Uses the rational method.

- Simple projects can be evaluated with an available free demonstration version.

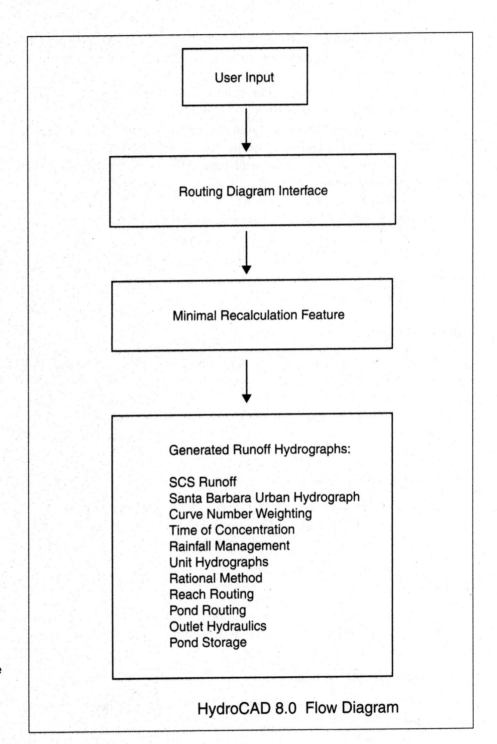

HydroCAD computer software allows users to model stormwater flows and create runoff hydrographs. *Balmori Associates.*

- More complex developments will need one of the paid versions, which allow subdividing a project into a number of subwatershed drainage areas.

- The HydroCAD website is www.hydrocad.net.

TR-55

- A somewhat more complicated model developed and supported by the Natural Resources Conservation Service (NRCS).

- Takes into account the time water takes to flow across the landscape, soil types, slopes, channel characteristics, and the presence and size of wetlands.

- Suitable only for small watersheds (those for which water travel times are 10 hours or less).

- Available for free download from www.wcc.nrcs.usda.gov/hydro/hydro-tools-models-wintr55.html.

HEC-1 (Hydrologic Engineering Center)

- Supported by the Army Corps of Engineers.

- Used for computing flood hydrographs in streams and rivers. (A storm hydrograph is the name given to the rapid rise and gradual decline in flow in a river caused by rainstorms.)

- Available for free download from www.hec.usace.army.mil/software/legacysoftware/hec1/hec1-download.htm.

Stormwater Quality

Virtually all stormwater quality models also predict runoff amounts. Nearly all are too complex for inexperienced users.

QUAL2K

- The stream water quality model of the EPA. An earlier version was called QUAL2E.

- Works in the Windows environment and with Excel spreadsheet data input.

- Among the easiest water quality models to use:

- Best suited to prediction of interactions among nutrients, dissolved oxygen, and algae.

- Has limited flexibility.

- Available for free download from www.epa.gov/ATHENS/wwqtsc/html/qual2k.html.

MOUSE

- Models surface runoff, open channel flow, pipe flow, water quality, and sediment transport for urban drainage systems, stormwater sewers, and sanitary sewers.

- A proprietary product, available for a fee from the DHI Software Mouse website, www.dhisoftware.com/mouse/ index.htm.

Hydrological Simulation Program—Fortran (HSPF)

- Supported by the USGS and EPA.

- A complex model that simulates surface runoff, snowmelt, evapotranspiration, groundwater recharge, baseflow, sediment, bacteria, temperature, pesticides, pH, and nutrients, among other parameters.

- Can be used at scales from a few acres to large river basins.

- Available for free download from http://water.usgs.gov/software/hspf .html.

Better Assessment Science Integrating Point and Nonpoint Sources (BASINS)

- Supported by the EPA.

- A multipurpose environmental analysis system for use by regional, state, and local agencies in performing watershed and water-quality-based studies.

- Works within an ArcView GIS system.

- Allows the quick assessment of large amounts of point source and nonpoint source data.

- HSPF and QUAL2E are sometimes used within this model.

- Very large-scale, thus is not appropriate for most land development.

- Available for download from the U.S. EPA. BASINS website, www.epa .gov/OST/BASINS.

Soil Water Assessment Tool (SWAT)

- Supported by the USDA.

- Evaluates flow and water quality at the river basin scale.

- Available for free download from www.brc.tamus.edu/swat/soft_model .html.

Stormwater Management Model (SWMM)

- Supported by the EPA.

- Used for analysis of quantity and quality problems related to stormwater runoff, combined sewers, sanitary sewers, and other drainage systems in urban areas, with many applications in nonurban areas as well.

- Also used for planning, design, and areawide control and impact assessment.

- Data intensive and requires validation.

- Available for download from the U.S. EPA, Urban Watershed Management Branch, SWMM Model website, www.epa.gov/ednnrmrl/swmm/ index.htm.

PCSWMM

- Utilizes the EPA SWMM core processes to provide a powerful geographic information system (GIS) with optional links to existing GIS/ AM/FM/CAD databases. PCSWMM is used as a decision support system for EPA SWMM.

- Available from the Computational Hydraulics, Inc. PCSWMM website, www. computationalhydraulics.com/pcswmmoverview.html.

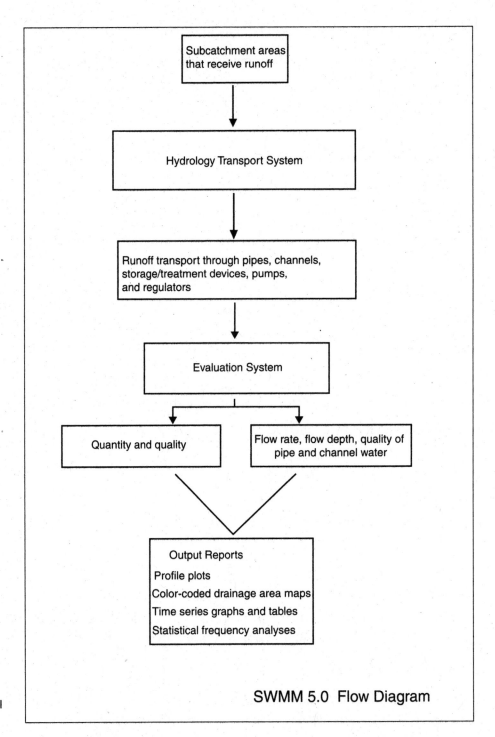

The EPA's Storm Water Management Model (SWMM) computer software is used by engineers and consultants to simulate both runoff quantity and quality for different rainfall events. *Balmori Associates.*

Soil Erosion

Universal Soil Loss Equation (USLE/RUSLE [Revised])

- Predicts erosion rates.

- Developed by the USDA (Science and Education Administration 1978).

- A simple empirical model based on an enormous amount of observational data.

- Can be employed by inexperienced users.

- Developed for agricultural fields, but can be applied—with caution—to other land uses, especially construction sites.

- Based on the formula $A = R \times K \times LS \times C \times P$, where: A is soil loss, R is a rainfall-runoff erosivity factor, K is a soil erodibility factor, LS is a slope length/steepness factor, C is a cover management factor, and P is a support practice factor. All factors are based on simple measurements of the site, or can be looked up in tables.

- A copy of the report (USDA Handbook 537) describing the model and its use, including data tables and figures, is available from http://topsoil.nserl.purdue.edu/usle/index.html.

Wind/Air

Windrose Plots (WRPLOT View)

- Based on WRPLOT, developed by the EPA.

- Generates quantitative graphical wind roses for any location.

- Easily used by novices.

- Uses meteorological data readily available on the Internet.

- Available as a free download from www.weblakes.com/lakewrpl.html.

Conjunction of Multizone Infiltration Specialists (COMIS)

- Models the airflow and contaminant distributions in buildings.

- Simulation Studio is COMIS with a user interface for UNIX or Windows computers.

- Available from the University of California, Lawrence Berkeley Laboratory, Energy Performance of Buildings Group, COMIS website, http://epb1.lbl.gov/comis.

Lighting

Advanced Daylighting and Electric Lighting Integrated New Environment (ADELINE)

- Provides information about the behavior and performance of indoor lighting systems, both natural and electrical.

- Requires a user fee.

- Available from Fraunhofer-Institut für Bauphysik, ADELINE website, www.ibp.fhg.de/wt/adeline/index.html.

Energy

Biogas!

- Allows calculation of design and characteristics of small biogas plants.

- Users must pay a license fee.

- Available from www.softplus.net/industrie/biogas/dateien.htm.

DOE-2

- Calculates the hourly energy use and energy cost of a commercial or residential building given information about the building's climate, construction, operation, utility rate schedule and heating, ventilating, and air-conditioning (HVAC) equipment.

- eQUEST and PowerDOE are other, more user-friendly versions of this software.

- A license fee is required.

- Available from the University of California, Lawrence Berkeley Laboratory, Building Energy Analysis, Simulation Research Group DOE-2 website, http://gundog.lbl.gov/dirsoft/d2whatis.html.

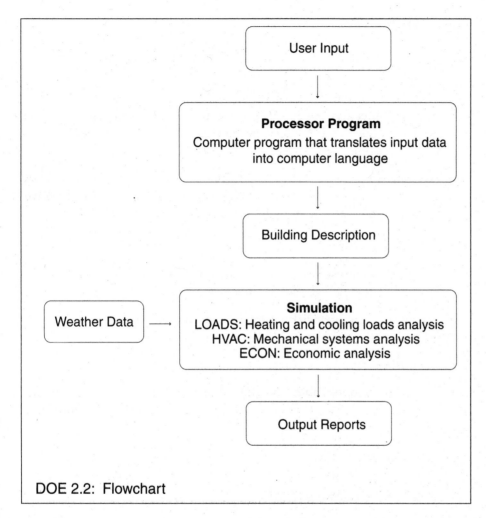

DOE 2.2: Flowchart

DOE-2.2 is a building energy analysis computer program that can predict the energy use and energy cost for all types of buildings. *Balmori Associates. Adapted from James Hirsch, 1998–2006.*

EnergyPlus

- A building energy simulation program for modeling building heating, cooling, lighting, ventilating, and other energy flows.

- Reads input and writes output to text files. Better to use one of several user interfaces that have been developed for this program.

- Supported by the U.S. Department of Energy.

- Information is available at the Energy Efficiency and Renewable Energy, Energy Plus website, www.eere.energy.gov/buildings/energyplus.

Home Energy Saver

- Free interactive Web-based tool for calculating energy use in residential buildings.

- Sponsored by the U.S. Department of Energy and the U.S. Environmental Protection Agency (EPA), as part of the national ENERGY STAR Program (Science To Achieve Results) for improving energy efficiency in homes.

- Available at the University of California, Lawrence Berkeley Laboratory, Environmental Energy Technologies Division, Home Energy Saver website, http://homeenergysaver.lbl.gov.

ProForm

- Provides a basic assessment of the environmental and financial impacts of renewable energy and energy efficiency projects.

- Calculates basic financial indicators and avoided emissions of CO_2 and local air pollutants expected from a project.

- Spreadsheet based.

- Free download available from the University of California, Lawrence Berkeley Laboratory, ProForm website, http://poet.lbl.gov/Proform.

Transportation

TRANsportation PLANning (TRANPLAN)

- Set of integrated programs that encompass the four-step travel demand model of trip generation, trip distribution, mode choice, and trip assignment for both highway and transit systems.

- A license fee is required.

- Available from www.citilabs.com/tranplan.

Urban Transportation Planning System (UTPS)

- System of analytical tools and methods developed by the Urban Mass Transportation Administration of the United States Department of Transportation in the 1970s.

The Herman Miller furniture manufacturing and assembly plant project began by grading the 22–acre building site to direct the drainage from the site's runoff from impervious surfaces into constructed wetlands and meadows. In order to manage the runoff from the 330,000-square-foot factory and the 12.7 acres of road and parking lot pavement, the 550-car parking lot was divided into three drainage sections, thereby dividing and dispersing both the volume and peak discharge loads of stormwater runoff. Constructed wetland meadows of grasses, forbs, sedges, and borders by hedgerows of floodplain trees were designed to capture stormwater runoff and both purify the water and allow for on–site infiltration.

This bioengineered hydrologic management system formed the foundation for the project's landscape design. The parking lot was reimagined as an integral part of an ecosystem rather than a barrier to healthy ecological processes: the wetland sections act in conjunction with the nearby parking lot strips to purify water, capture stormwater runoff, prevent erosion, and add and maintain wildlife habitat on–site. The integration of constructed ecological systems

This aerial view of the Herman Miller factory under construction shows how the parking areas—integrated with the wetlands—became part of a thriving ecological system by capturing runoff and creating wildlife habitat. *Michael Van Valkenburgh Associates, Inc.*

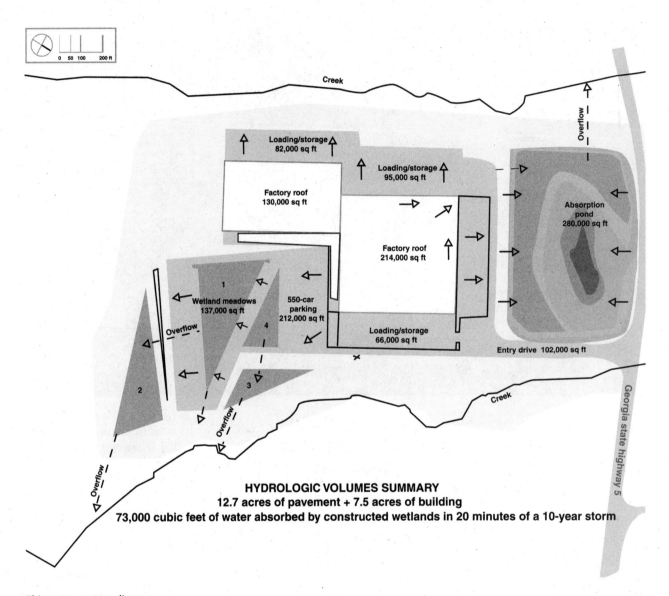

0 50 100   200 ft

Creek

Overflow

Loading/storage
82,000 sq ft

Loading/storage
95,000 sq ft

Factory roof
130,000 sq ft

Absorption
pond
280,000 sq ft

Factory roof
214,000 sq ft

1

Wetland meadows
137,000 sq ft

550-car
parking
212,000 sq ft

4

Loading/storage
66,000 sq ft

Overflow

Entry drive 102,000 sq ft

2

3

Overflow

Creek

Georgia state highway 5

Overflow

HYDROLOGIC VOLUMES SUMMARY
12.7 acres of pavement + 7.5 acres of building
73,000 cubic feet of water absorbed by constructed wetlands in 20 minutes of a 10-year storm

This water system diagram maps and calculates the flows of this stormwater volume into the Herman Miller parking lot wetland meadows and absorptive pond. *Michael Van Valkenburgh Associates, Inc.*

into human-use areas also created a more satisfying arrival and departure experience for factory employees.

The 70-acre rural Georgia-based site for the Herman Miller plant required 10 acres of parking space, but the project's economic budget did not include landscape architecture in the business plan. Michael Van Valkenburgh Associates convinced the client to redirect funds from the engineering

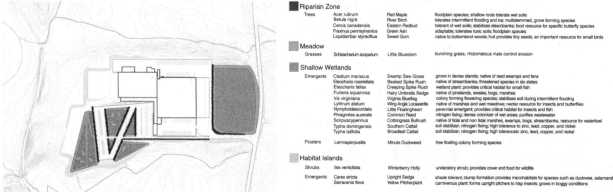

Riparian Zone			
Trees	Acer rubrum	Red Maple	floodplain species; shallow roots tolerate wet soils
	Betula nigra	River Birch	tolerates intermittent flooding and ice; multistemmed, grove forming species
	Cercis canadensis	Eastern Redbud	tolerant of wet soils; stabilizes steambanks; food resource for specific butterfly species
	Fraxinus pennsylvanica	Green Ash	adaptable; tolerates toxic soils; floodplain species
	Liquidambar styraciflua	Sweet Gum	native to bottomland woods; fruit provides tiny seeds, an important resource for small birds
Meadow			
Grasses	Schizacharium scoparium	Little Bluestem	bunching grass, rhizomatous mats control erosion
Shallow Wetlands			
Emergents	Cladium mariscus	Swamp Saw Grass	grows in dense stands; native of reed swamps and fens
	Eleocharis rosetellata	Beaked Spike Rush	native of streambanks; threatened species in six states
	Eleocharis fallax	Creeping Spike Rush	wetland plant; provides critical habitat for small fish
	Furiena squarrosa	Hairy Umbrella Sedge	native of pinelands, swales, bogs, marshes
	Iris virginica	Virginia Blueflag	colony forming flowering species; stabilizes soil during intermittent flooding
	Lythrum alatum	Wing Angle Loosestrife	native of marshes and wet meadows; nectar resource for insects and butterflies
	Nymphoidescordata	Little Floatingheart	perennial emergent; provides critical habitat for insects and fish
	Phragmites australis	Common Reed	nitrogen fixing; dense colonizer of wet areas; purifies wastewater
	Scirpuscyperinus	Cottongrass Bullrush	native of tidal and non tidal marshes, swamps, bogs, streambanks, resource for waterfowl
	Typha domingensis	Southern Cattail	soil stabilizer; nitrogen fixing; high tolerance to zinc, lead, copper, and nickel
	Typha latifolia	Broadleaf Cattail	soil stabilizer; nitrogen fixing; high toleranceto zinc, lead, copper, and nickel
Floaters	Lemnaperpusilla	Minute Duckweed	free floating colony forming species
Habitat Islands			
Shrubs	Ilex verticillata	Winterberry Holly	understory shrub; provides cover and food for wildlife
Emergents	Carex stricta	Upright Sedge	shade tolerant; clump formation provides microhabitats for species such as duckwee, salamanders
	Sarracenia flava	Yellow Pitcherplant	carniverous plant; forms upright pitchers to trap insects; grows in boggy conditions

budget to use for grading and bioengineering as a way to integrate stormwater management into an industrial landscape in a model of environmental stewardship.

The integration of natural processes into a factory landscape and industrial-scale parking lot is a model of ecologically responsible stormwater management that could be applied to many urban and suburban development projects.

The Herman Miller factory's 550-car parking lot was divided into three drainage sections, where stormwater runoff is captured by absorptive plant habitats transitioning from a riparian zone of floodplain trees into a meadow and wetland. *Michael Van Valkenburgh Associates, Inc.*

Whitney Water Purification Facility and Park, New Haven, Connecticut

CREDITS: The Bioengineering Group, Inc. (Site Hydraulic and Wetland Engineer), Michael Van Valkenburgh Associates, Inc. (Landscape Architect), Steven Holl Architects (Architect), CH2Mhill (Water Treatment Processing and HVAC engineer)

HIGHLIGHT: A working landscape

Perhaps the real significance of this project lies in the fact that an infrastructure facility dropped in the middle of a residential enclave in the outskirts of New Haven, Connecticut, received a high level of design in its architecture (Steven Holl), landscape architecture (M. Van Valkenburgh), and hydraulic engineering (The Bioengineering Group). Although this project has become a poster child for water treatment, its status has been diminished by recent events. Conceived as an educational facility and park, post-9/11 fears have required that it be made into a secluded private facility, allowing no public access to its building, only to its park.

The story of the treatment of water on-site is the other point of interest. The water purification plant is built on a 14-acre site, on land originally purchased by Eli Whitney in 1798 (the site still has the original Whitney barn and colonial house). This purification plant cleans 15 million gallons of water a day. The purification facilities are placed beneath the landscaped park, with the operational programs above, in a 360-foot-long stainless steel tubelike body, which includes the lobby, laboratories, lecture hall, and operational facilities. The plant's energy source is a groundwater heat pump system of 88 wells, which provides a renewable energy source for heating and cooling the building.

The Bioengineering Group's integrated stormwater management system based the entire stormwater collection, conveyance, and treatment system on a natural hydrocycle approach. The design reduces runoff, infiltrates runoff close to the source, and keeps water in contact with vegetation and soils, to promote evapotranspiration and biogeochemical treatment of nutrients and other pollutants commonly carried in stormwater.

Much of the park grounds are covered with tall grasses that absorb water better than turfgrass. A green roof reduces annual runoff volume by 70 percent, and reproduces runoff curves for a meadow for storms up to 5 inches in magnitude. Vegetated swales throughout the site converge to form a stream channel that leads to the stormwater management pond with wetland borders.

Vegetated swales converge at a pond and wetland in front of the building, purifying and storing both stormwater and graywater on site. *Photo by Diana Balmori.*

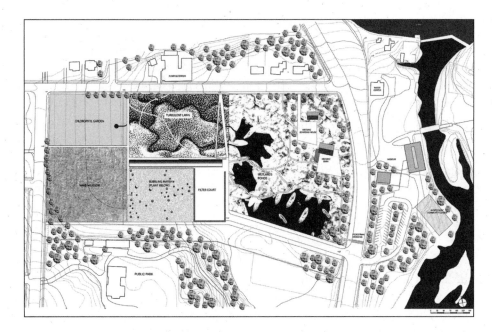

The landscape design is based on the six stages of the water purification process. The park itself acts as a natural filtration system. © 2005 Steven Holl Architects.

The flow of the stream is augmented by water discharged from the deep foundation drain. The site actually releases the same quality and quantity of water to the Mill River as if the entire site were covered by a forest.

The project is designed to manage water as a valuable natural resource, with the water removed from the deep foundation being pumped into the vegetated bioretention swales, rather than sewer drains as usual. The flushing water for the treatment plan is also directed to the landscape drainage features where it sustains the wetland habitats on-site. Stormwater generated from built surfaces is not piped off-site, but conserved for the productive supply of aquatic conditions in swales, wetlands, and the pond. The bioretention swales feature native wet meadow plantings, while the bordering vegetated wetlands surrounding the pond host emergent wetland plantings and a dense riparian shrub buffer zone. The pond itself is designed to maintain deep areas of standing water that support mosquito-eating fish for natural pest control. The pond has intricate and diverse grading and plantings to enhance edge habitat and diverse physical niches for aquatic organisms. All this was made visible by the design to serve as an educational landscape about water.

The site creates an assemblage of new habitats linked by their stormwater management capacities. Quality habitat is essential for the many migratory birds that also use the nearby park, seen in the background. © 2005 Steven Holl Architects (Chris McVoy).

Sidwell Friends School, Washington, D.C.

CREDITS: Andropogon Associates, Ltd. (Landscape Architect), Natural Systems International (Wastewater Engineer), Bruce Brooks & Associates (Mechanical and Electrical Engineer), CVM Engineers (Structural Engineer), VIKA, Inc. (Civil Engineer), Kieran Timberlake Associates, LLP (Architect)

HIGHLIGHT: Site wastewater treatment as educational tool for a school

The school administrators, in the midst of renovating and expanding facilities at its Washington, DC, campus, wished to make building and landscape sustainable systems visible on their campus and use these practices as an educational tool. To that end, the design by Andropogon includes a rain garden, an on-site wastewater treatment (a system akin to the Living Machine), a green roof, solar panels and native plantings.

The wetlands-based treatment system cleans sewage and sink water from the building. Sewage receives primary treatment in an underground tank, then is recirculated through terraced reed beds. Microorganisms there break down water contaminants. A trickle filter and sand filter follow. The outflow is recycled into the building for reuse in toilets. The system is used as a teaching tool for the science program.

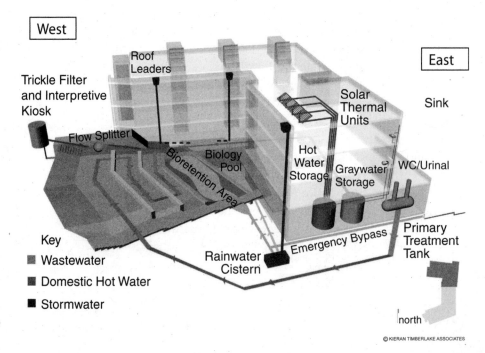

This diagram maps the flows and storage areas of wastewater, domestic hot water, and stormwater systems in the Sidwell Friends building and landscape. © 2004 Kieran Timberlake Associates, LLP.

The proposed middle school courtyard includes both a wastewater and stormwater management system: the pond and rain garden capture and retain stormwater runoff, while the wetlands process wastewater from the building. The visibility of the water management systems in the landscape allows these systems to be educational tools. *Drawing by Andropogon Associates, Ltd., and Kieran Timberlake Associates.*

Drawing by Andropogon Associates Ltd. and Kieran Timberlake Associates

1. Existing middle school
2. Middle school addition
3. Trickle filter with interpretive display
4. Wetlands for wastewater treatment
5. Rain garden
6. Pond

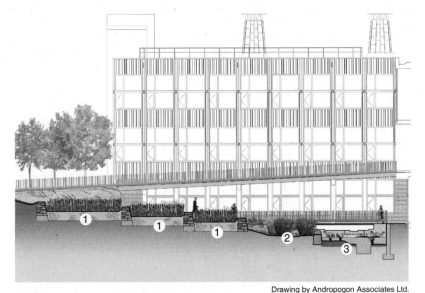

Drawing by Andropogon Associates Ltd.

1. Wetlands for wastewater treatment
2. Rain garden
3. Pond

There is an aesthetic continuity between the (1) wetlands, (2) rain gardens, and (3) pond, but the wastewater and stormwater management systems have separate water flows. *Drawing by Andropogon Associates, Ltd.*

In addition, stormwater runoff is directed to a rain garden and biology pond. Runoff from the roof is collected in an underground cistern that maintains the water levels of the pond in dry periods. The water from storms accumulates in the rain gardens and seeps slowly into the ground, being cleaned in the process.

The plantings reflect the plant communities of the soil moisture gradient: emergent aquatics, wet meadow species, and upland species at the perimeter.

Meadow Creek Watershed Restoration at the University of Virginia (UVA), Charlottesville, Virginia

CREDITS: Judith Nitsch Engineering, Inc. (Engineer), Nelson Byrd Woltz Landscape Architects (Landscape Architect), PHR&A Engineering, Inc. (Engineer), Biohabitats, Inc. (Hydrologist)

HIGHLIGHT: Campus development and restoration of its stream as stormwater management

The west side of UVA's campus planned new development made the issue of stormwater management and the effect on the stream that runs through it—Meadow Creek—critical to its implementation.

Meadow Creek was a degraded stream, so the solutions needed to address its restoration and offer management solutions for its 850-acre watershed, rather than address individual projects and their individual impact.

One of the three regional stormwater mitigation sites identified in the Meadow Creek Regional Stormwater Management Plan, prepared by Judith Nitsch Engineering, is the Dell, which will be looked at in more detail here (the other two are the Emmet Street Garage and the multipurpose arena, described more briefly later).

In the Dell, the solutions included 1,100 linear feet of new streambank; the creation of wetlands and a new pond as a landscape feature; a sediment area before entering the pond; and biofiltration islands and vegetated filters. All help restore the stream. They also serve to mitigate UVA's dozens of developments in the Meadow Creek watershed, fulfilling its obligations to the regional stormwater management plan.

Here is a brief description of the two other regional stormwater mitigation sites:

- *Multipurpose arena:* This 15,000-seat arena is another of the new projects built by the university within the Meadow Creek watershed. Rather than being treated as an individual project, it is part of the overall management

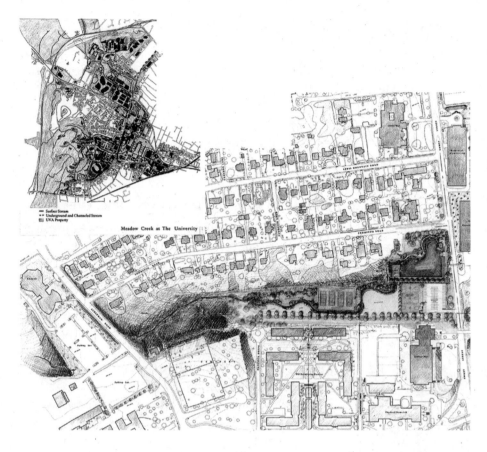

A plan view showing the restoration of Meadow Creek at the University of Virginia, Charlottesville, which included the daylighting of 1,200 linear feet of a previously piped stream, wetlands creation, and a new stormwater basin. © *2003 Nelson Byrd Woltz Landscape Architects.*

The newly daylighted Meadow Creek flows to a waterfall into a forebay, where sediments settle out. A weir in the stone wall controls flow from the forebay into the pond, where biofiltration islands and vegetated filters uptake nutrients and pollutants. © *2005 Nelson Byrd Woltz Landscape Architects.*

plan. Streambank/floodway restoration, created wetlands and ponds, biofiltration islands, and vegetated filters were all part of the solution.

- *Emmet Street Garage:* This 1,200-car garage was the third mitigation site in the Meadow Creek watershed where streambank/floodway relocation took place, otherwise following the regional plan.

The projects developed here all received individual solutions, but they fit into an overall plan.

The Oregon Museum of Science and Industry's bioswales capture suspended solids, pollutants, and rainwater on-site, as well as aesthetically connect the parking lot to the nearby riverfront. *Scott Murase.*

Oregon Museum of Science and Industry (OMSI), Portland, Oregon

CREDITS: Murase Associates (Landscape Architects), Zimmer Gunsul Frasca Partnership (Architect), Portland Bureau of Environmental Services (Project Support)

HIGHLIGHT: Parking lot stormwater management

OMSI calls itself a nonprofit educational and entertainment center in Portland, Oregon. The site was developed as a science park and provided an opportunity to clean up a wasted site and add vitality to the riverfront. Its parking lot bioswales are Portland's first large on-site stormwater and infiltration project.

The runoff from 4 acres of the 6-acre parking lot is collected in 10 different bioswales. Their overflow enters a storm sewer system, which drains to an outfall to the Willamette River. Before the creation of these swales, more than 522,000 cubic feet of untreated stormwater runoff went directly to the river. Though the system was designed mainly to filter pollutants, the swales also provide good infiltration (they infiltrate at the rate of 8 inches per hour).

In reviewing redevelopment plans for OMSI, the Portland Bureau of Environmental Services (BES) came up with the idea of asking OMSI to voluntarily redesign the parking lots and the landscape to treat pollutants in stormwater runoff. (There were no regulations at the time.) OMSI agreed.

The swales, 10 total, are 6 feet wide and vary in length from 100 to 250 feet. Wooden check dams were installed every 50 feet to slow the flows and encourage infiltration. Finally, one 12-inch-wide curb cut every 30 feet allowed water to enter the swales from the parking lot surface.

The bioswales eliminated the need for stormwater pipes, sedimentation manholes, and catch basins, allowing the developer to save $78,000 in construction costs in spite of additional design fees. The system is being used as a model for applying biofiltration technology in urban waste water management.

Because this project is 16 years old and has been monitored and modified in response to observation over time, the project has been able to record some lessons learned.

The following alterations were recommended:

- Some curb cuts do not allow enough water from the parking lot to enter the swales, due to the buildup of sediments, which blocks runoff from entering the swales.

- The performance of the swales could be improved by increasing the number of curb cuts from one every 30 feet on center, to one every 10 feet on center. This minor change would prevent the short-circuiting of runoff from the swales.

- Because the bioswales were oversized, the 12-inch freeboard originally specified in the plans to accommodate the peak storm runoff volume was not necessary.

- Thick painted stripes across the parking area pavement could help divert runoff into the curb cuts more efficiently.

- Grading paved areas to facilitate perpendicular flow into curb cuts is the most efficient design.

Smaller parking lot stalls allowed the Oregon Museum of Science and Industry to free up space for the almost 14,000 square feet of bioswales designed to capture runoff from the 800-car parking lot. *Scott Murase.*

Ray and Maria Stata Center at Massachusetts Institute of Technology (MIT), Cambridge, Massachusetts

CREDITS: Frank Gehry Partners, LLP (Architect), Cannon Design (Associate Architect), Olin Partnership (Landscape Architect), Judith Nitsch Engineering, Inc. (Engineer), R. G.

Vegetation filters water as it moves down toward a wetland and an underground storage cell. *Image courtesy of Judith Nitsch Engineering, Inc.*

Vanderweil Engineers, Inc. (MEP Engineer), John A. Martin and Associates, Inc. (Structural Engineer)

HIGHLIGHT: Stormwater harvesting on a dense urban campus

The 713,000-square foot Computer, Information and Intelligence Sciences building, by Frank Gehry, includes a main building and two levels of below-grade parking. In a tight urban campus site, the project managed to develop several sustainable site systems and a stormwater management system. The landscape architects' (Olin Partnership) design for the site is a New England–like landscape of simulated glacial elements such as drumlins and outwash features. The engineers (JNEI) activated the landscape forms to carry out particular hydrological functions.

Green design elements include runoff storage in landforms, created wetlands to improve stormwater quality, water harvesting for toilet flushing, solar-powered pumping for stormwater quality, and irrigation of the wetland area. The green elements of this landscape were integrated into this very tight urban campus.

Emerald Square Mall, North Attleboro, Massachusetts

CREDITS: Sumner Schein Architects & Engineers, Inc. (Architect), Anderson-Nichols, Inc. (Engineer), IEP, Inc. (Engineering Consultant), GZA GeoEnvironmental Technologies, Inc. (Engineering Consultant), New England Development (Developer)

HIGHLIGHT: A regional mall built upstream from a water supply reservoir

A developer identified a prime location for a regional mall at the intersection of two interstate highways north of Providence, Rhode Island. The problem was that it sat within the watershed of the Sevenmile River, a tributary for a drinking water reservoir of the city of North Attleboro. Malls have large impervious parking lots with clearly negative consequences for water quality and flow characteristics. The 1,000,000-square-foot mall could not be built unless it could be shown that there would be no negative impact on water quality in the Sevenmile River.

In 1991, the developer hired the IEP consulting engineering firms to design a system to handle and purify stormwater from the mall roof and parking lot. The engineers began with a detailed hydrologic model of the site. Because of its topography and large surface area, the 60-acre site was divided into two subwatersheds, with approximately half of the flow diverted to each

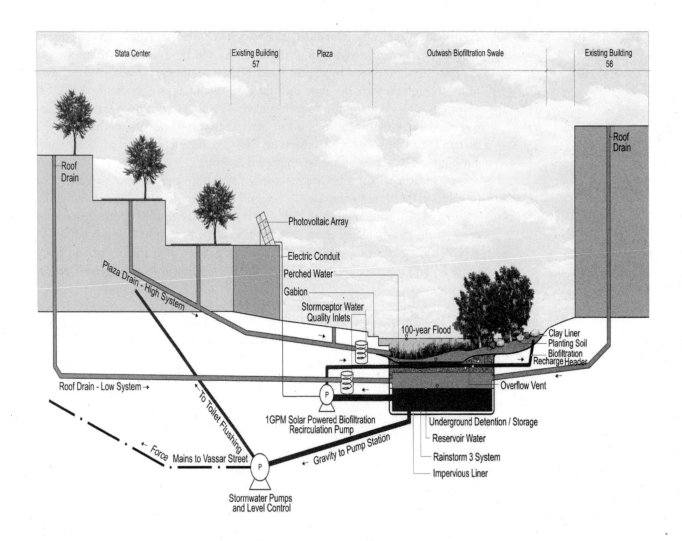

Stata Center Stormwater Schematic Cross-Section

of two treatment systems. Each treatment system began with a settling basin designed to allow 24-hour residence time for the entire volume of a one-year recurrence interval storm. The design called for the ponds to be dredged whenever they fill in 25 percent, to restore their capacity, but that has not been required as of the time of this writing. Dredging will help to protect the downstream constructed wetlands from siltation.

Outflow from each settling/detention pond passes to a constructed wetland designed as a series of subbasins that maximize water residence time and

A schematic diagram of the stormwater system shows how water is harvested, biofiltered, stored, and reused for toilet flushing. Water moves by gravity and by solar-powered pumps. *Image courtesy of Judith Nitsch Engineering, Inc.*

treatment effectiveness. Each of the two wetlands has a total area of about 1 acre. The design is standard, with an excavated basin lined with an impermeable barrier covered by organic soil. They operate as free water surface systems, though they are dry much of the year. Originally vegetated with 30,000 plantings, natural plant communities have taken over with no negative consequences. They require almost no maintenance. One added benefit is that the wetlands can be closed off, blocking flow in the event of an unlikely catastrophic spill, such as an overturned tanker truck.

In addition to these structural measures, a number of best management practices (BMPs) are employed. These include weekly sweeping of the parking lots to remove contaminated dust and dry deposition, frequent cleaning of catch basins to maintain their capacity, and use of calcium-based road salt to avoid sending excess sodium to the reservoir. The catch basins are equipped with oil and grease traps to reduce pollutant loading to the treatment ponds and wetlands.

The treatment wetlands were allowed to operate for two years before the mall was built, to allow them to reach a natural equilibrium. This also allowed them to serve as treatment systems during the construction phase of the mall.

Permitting requires frequent monitoring of water quality of the effluent leaving the wetlands. The treatment systems have been a great success, and average levels of suspended solids, nutrients, oil and grease, metals, and organics have consistently fallen well below NPDES limits. The drainage area of the treatment systems happens to pick up a portion of the exit ramp for the adjoining highway, an area not on the mall property. Because the wetlands treat runoff from this unassociated nonpoint source that used to flow directly to the Sevenmile, the engineers believe water quality in the river may actually have improved since the mall was built.

Environmental sensitivity and cooperation with regulators, coupled with careful design allowed a regional mall to be built at a prime location where it otherwise would have been prevented.

Energy

Butterfield Luton Commercial Park, Butterfield, England

CREDITS: Atelier Ten UK (Environmental Consultant), Hamilton Associates (Architect), BEA Landscape Design (Landscape Architect)

HIGHLIGHT: Earth ducts for air cooling and warming

The cooling system of this English development, in the village of Butterfield, has a singular characteristic that is the reason for its inclusion in this text: it uses earth ducts. The large site is put to work to deliver a project low in energy use. The Butterfield scheme is a development by the Easter Group on a Greenfield site in northeast Luton, England, for a technology business park with a total floor area in excess of 1,000,000 square feet. The site master plan consists mainly of offices, laboratories, and smaller businesses targeting technology start-ups in units ranging from 2,000 to 5,000 square feet, located in the heart of the development. The broad scope of the project allows for an overall approach and would be very difficult if tackled building by building.

The buildings in Butterfield's Business Village have an innovative passive heating and cooling ventilation system using earth ducts, which will reduce energy consumption by up to 75 percent and regulate air temperature. Butterfield's earth duct system will draw fresh air into the buildings via raised intake grilles in the landscape and through 260-foot-long (80-meter) concrete pipes, or earth ducts, which will be buried below the buildings and landscape.

The earth ducts bring the incoming air into contact with the thermal mass of the earth, which provides "free" preheating in the winter and cooling in the summer, thus maintaining a more steady air temperature supply to the building. In the summer, the earth will cool the air before it is introduced to the building. In the winter, the cold air will be warmed by the ground before passing over a small heating panel fed from the boiler to bring the air up to room temperature on very cold days.

Fresh air is drawn down into the earth duct, where contact with the thermal mass of the earth provides preheating and cooling. The pressurized floor plenum supplies the air to the office space above. *Atelier Ten UK.*

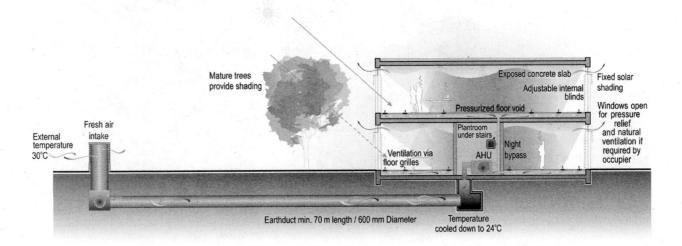

An integrated landscape drainage system, with swales and balancing ponds, will help to manage surface water runoff, reduce peak flows, and limit the risk of flooding, while providing a more attractive environment and creating natural wildlife habitat areas.

Butterfield has been designed to fit around existing mature hedgerows and areas of boundary woodland, each of which has specific associated wildlife. The landscape is designed to be natural in order to encourage a wide variety of species to flourish: wildflower meadows and grassed areas, with more formal ornamental planting close to buildings.

The environmental engineer Patrick Bellow, who heads Atelier Ten UK in England, has compared the earth duct system to termite hills in Africa as a forerunner from the natural world (see illustration) and to some Palladian villas in Italy on hills, which used a related way of earth cooling.

Termite mounds take advantage of the earth's natural tendency to stay cool during the day to push hot air out of the core. *Left: Atelier Ten UK. Right: © 2006 Shirley Grant.*

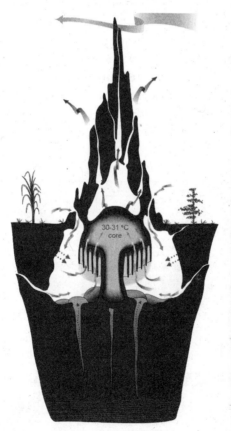

Institute for Forestry and Nature Research ("Alterra") in Wageningen, the Netherlands

CREDITS: Copijn Utrecht (Landscape Architect), Aronsohn V.O.F. (Structural Engineer), Deerns R.I. (Mechanical Engineer), Behnisch & Behnisch, Architects (now: Behnisch Architekten) (Architect)

HIGHLIGHT: Greenhouses as microclimate creators for a project

The design and planning of the new building and site for the Institute for Forestry and Nature Research, now called "Alterra," were the result of a competition at the invitation of the Dutch state building department (Rijksgebouwendienst).

The site, an overfertilized cornfield, was not in line with the ecological aims of the project. Therefore, the cornfield was treated to be able to develop on its own over the years.

In summer, sunlight increases evaporation of the pond water, which keeps temperatures cool. The large volume of air in the glass houses helps to balance indoor and outdoor temperatures. *Professor Christian Kandzia.*

The building is shaped like an E, with two glazed gardens between the offices in the three "fingers." The glass houses are the central element of the climatic concept, acting as heat buffers and shading elements with plants, improving the microclimate. The heat from the façades is collected in these glass houses. The large air volume of the roofed garden balances outdoor and indoor temperature differences. In winter, the diffuse sunlight heats the large volumes of the glass houses very quickly, turning them into comfortable and usable spaces. During the summer they collect the sunlight, which increases the evaporation of water from the ponds and the leaves of the plants, thus reducing the air temperature in the glass houses.

With the exception of a few special areas, none of the spaces are air conditioned. The comfort is achieved by a carefully elaborated natural climatic

In winter, the glass houses trap diffuse sunlight, quickly warming the room. *Professor Christian Kandzia.*

The exterior features a much more naturalized landscape than its previous existence as an overfertilized cornfield. *Professor Christian Kandzia.*

strategy making optimum use of the glass houses, which act as climate buffers between interior and exterior spaces.

This is conservation design through the use of glass houses, which are also beautiful spaces in common for all the building users. It is curious, however, that water management has not been made part of the equation and that the exterior—the former cornfield—has not been engaged in this function either. Its transformation from over-fertilized field to a *laissez faire* return to whatever grows on it has not been actively engaged through plantings that can return the soil's health.

Infrastructure as Public Space

Prairie Waterway, Farmington, Minnesota

CREDITS: Rodney Hardy, Sienna Development Corporation (Developer), Balmori Associates, Inc. (Landscape and Environmental Design), Paul Barten, Yale School of Forestry and Environmental Studies (Hydrologist), Glenn Cook, Bonestroo, Rosene, Anderlik & Associates, Inc. (Engineer and Architect), William Morrish, Design Center for American Urban Landscape (Advisor), Lee Smick, City Planner for Farmington, Minnesota

HIGHLIGHT: Water infrastructure as public park

The Farmington, Minnesota, waterway is designed with a suburban housing development of 486 midpriced homes built by the Sienna Development Corporation of Minneapolis. The project grew out of the desire to try a different approach to standard drainage systems. The Farmington waterway is created as a drainage system alternative to the usual underground straight-line water pipe. It functions successfully as a drainage project, as demonstrated during the recent peak flooding years of 1998 and 2001, when the Mississippi River crested and remained above its floodplain for at least three months in each of those years. In addition, and perhaps more important, the project creates public space—a park—as part of the drainage solution.

Farmington, a small farming town, is about 25 miles northwest of Minneapolis, close enough to the nearby urban area to create a high demand for housing. Rod Hardy, director of the Sienna Development Corporation, proposed building a development of some 500 houses over the course of 10 to 15 years, with the initial phase totaling approximately 170 houses. In 1993, several months after the summer of the worst flooding of the Mississippi River in 20 years, William Moorish, director of the Center of American Urban Landscape at the University of Minnesota, proposed to the town that Balmori Associates design a different kind of drainage system for the planned Farmington Development, which the town had not approved at that point. The developers initial proposal was standard, directing

The waterway collects stormwater runoff from a new, large development, two former developments further south, and an agricultural field. *Photo by Bordner Aerials.*

the increased runoff into a single pipe, which would then empty into the nearby Vermillion River and continue on into the Mississippi River, about 20 miles from Farmington.

The town of Farmington made the development of an innovative drainage system a condition for approval of the development plan. The town planner, Lee Smick, supported the idea of a prairie waterway/park throughout the lengthy approval process; and the town board, comprising mostly local farmers, did not object, but expressed some degree of apprehension over the need to buy land exclusively for the water system. The land was purchased with city money recovered through taxes paid on the property once the houses had been sold (tax increment financing). The taxes were established by the town as contributions by the developer to provide needed facilities, but the city also had to buy additional land beyond the development to allow access for the water to flow to the Vermillion River.

The developers planned layout was modified by the landscape firm to reduce the stormwater runoff. Street widths were narrowed, driveways were shortened, and at the center of each block, a depression was made to gather the water from spring rains running off the roofs and lots. These latter areas at the center of each block were to be thickly planted with trees (e.g., red maples) that can survive with roots in standing water for part of the year. These trees, through their foliage (evapotranspiration), would get rid of the water in these depressions.

Planting turned out to be the most troublesome part of the project. Basically, neither the developer not the city had sufficient funds to allow planting the center of the blocks; the public green space created by the new water system was planted with very small trees to stretch the budget. Moreover, it was not possible to alter the house/lot layout.

Three separate water systems are used in the Farmington prairie waterway:

- A swale system to treat the stormwater runoff from the new housing development that lies immediately to the west of Park Place.

- A pond and channel system designed to move and clean the water over a large area before it enters the Vermillion River.

- Type I (periodically inundated) and Type II (sedge meadows) wetlands intended to make up for wetlands lost to the proposed development and to provide temporary storage for elevated groundwater levels.

Two housing developments to the south of the Park Place development in Farmington, Castle Rock, and Henderson were also served by the drainage system. Both new developments had drainage problems: basements in the homes flood each spring. Their stormwater enters the pond at the southern end of the Park Place site. The channel leaving the pond slows the water, which is cleansed as it moves through the vegetation. The great conductivity of the local soils means that groundwater rises and falls quickly during and after storm events. Under these circumstances, the wide width of the channel, which varies between 80 and 110 feet, helps to reduce the velocity and scouring of the waterway. The vegetated, expanded streambed traps particulates and takes up nutrients.

Finally, runoff from the Sienna Development housing itself is sent into stormwater swales just east of the neighborhood. These wide stormwater swales are set above the groundwater level and are temporarily inundated after a storm. The water moves very slowly southward over sedges and grasses that help to clean the water before it subsides or moves north through subsurface flow into the channel and onto the Vermillion River. This doubling-back of the water flow gives increased residence time, and therefore increased treatment before the water enters the channel. During periods of base flow, the water rises to fill a shelf on either side of it. The stormwater swales become inundated from both road runoff and the temporarily elevated groundwater. The water remains below the level of the recreational pathways and the upland edges of the park. In addition, the water has not spread overland into the mitigating wetlands.

Only in 100-year events is the berm between the wetlands and the channel breached. The berm separating the stormwater swales from the channel is set at an elevation that will keep them separate even during the 100-year event. On September 15, 1998, just as the construction of the drainage system was completed, a 100-year flood event took place. The drainage system worked exactly as it was supposed to, the berm was breached, and the mitigating wetlands stored the higher waters.

The Farmington housing development, started in 1990, was intended to be built in three five-year phases. The 486-unit housing development was finished in the fall of 2000 and was completely sold out by that time. Residents who purchased the $150,000 homes are pleased, not only because they do not have to worry about possible flood damage to their homes, but also because they can enjoy the beauty and proximity of the

The watercourse, lined with paths, creates a public amenity. *Photo by Bordner Aerials.*

park, pond system, and waterway at the edge of the development. Children play in the ponds and connecting streams. Fishermen catch bass. Families spread blankets for picnics near the water's edge. Joggers and cyclists frequently spot deer, woodpeckers, chipmunks, and other wildlife as they use the paved paths and green spaces. Residents renamed the project Park Place.

Riverbank State Park in Harlem, New York, New York

CREDITS: Endeco International (Developer), Abel Bainnson Butz, LLC (Landscape Architect), Richard Dattner & Partners Architects (Architect)

HIGHLIGHT: Infrastructure as the base for public space

A very large sewage plant on the Hudson River served as a platform for a new public park. The history of the sewage plant is a mixed one, as building it many decades ago took away green space from the neighborhood. It was started in 1972, stopped for 10 years, and finished in 1993. Undoubtedly, the 28-acre park was a deal sweetener to get the neighborhood to accept the sewage plant's presence. It required building pedestrian bridges at both ends, 138th and 145th Streets, spanning the Henry Hudson Parkway to give access to the park from the neighborhood. It has also meant a further investment to control the odor emanating from the plant, which has been subdued but is not gone.

In spite of these drawbacks, the plant has provided a 28-acre park on its roof with many great facilities, such as a 50-meter Olympic-size indoor swimming pool, not frequently found in New York City; an ice skating rink (for roller skating in the summer); a track surrounding a soccer field; four basketball courts; four handball courts; an amphitheater; a 25-meter outdoor

The roof of a sewage treatment plant on the Hudson River has been transformed into an amenity-rich urban park, reopening the waterfront to Harlem residents. *Imagery Copyright 2003 Getmapping Plc. www.getmapping.com.*

swimming pool; football and soccer fields; a carousel; tennis courts; and programs for children in swimming, art, ballet, karate, and ice skating. A community garden completes this lengthy list.

The considerable size and budgets of infrastructure projects make them worthy of working double duty by having them carry public space with them. It is not a path explored in public works much at all, nor is it considered in private developments. But as in an earlier example in this book of a drainage project for a new housing development in Farmington, Minnesota, made into a public park, it is a valuable strategy. In the earlier example, it was a way of making the project more sustainable. In the Harlem project, it could be argued that the sewage plant helps to keep the Hudson River clean. It is not, however, a new or more sustainable way of dealing with sewage; it is simply better than dumping raw sewage into the river.

The EPA provides grants for constructing sewage treatment plants with associated "aesthetic treatment." Generally, aesthetic treatment is limited to some sort of window-dressing (use a material in tune with the neighborhood, etc.). A sustainable reinterpretation would be to use such infrastructure pieces as launch pads for a new kind of public urban park.

Sustainable Suburbanism

Pennsylvania Growing Greener Program

CREDITS: The Natural Lands Trust, Pennsylvania Department of Conservation and Natural Resources (DCNR), Penn State Cooperative Extension Service

HIGHLIGHT: Conservation design versus cluster regulations

The work of Conservation Design in Pennsylvania purports to create different zoning approaches and to obtain better sustainable developments than those created by typical cluster regulations. It has been adopted by many communities in Pennsylvania, and the most important of the Conservation Design guidelines is that it gives municipal officials the ability to add land to an interconnected greenway system every time development occurs. It is beyond the scope of this text to describe in detail all the differences between cluster development and conservation design, but it has different zoning approaches and different subdivision regulations. Summarily, Conservation Design asks for a greater proportion of green public space in a development and attempts to have it connect with other green space in its vicinity. It sets up guidelines for the development to create new greenways, so it is a step closer to more sustainable systems than cluster development, which is characterized by Conservation Design as preserving the "ring around the collar" buffers and berms, which the group considers an antiquated approach (Ann Hutchinson, Natural Lands Trust. Personal communication.).

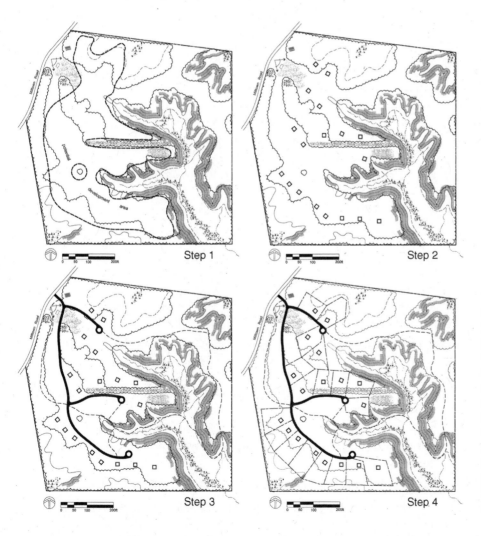

These diagrams outline the four-step process recommended by Growing Greener to plan and design a conservation subdivision that preserves natural features and open space: (1) locating possible areas of development; (2) siting houses; (3) creating transportation networks; and (4) dividing lots. *Drawings by Natural Lands Trust, Inc. From* Growing Greener *by Randall Arendt. © 1999 Natural Lands Trust. Reprinted by permission of Island Press.*

These diagrams show only three of the many options that conservation planning presents as alternatives to conventional planning. *Drawings by Natural Lands Trust, Inc. From* Growing Greener *by Randall Arendt.* © 1999 Natural Lands Trust. *Reprinted by permission of Island Press.*

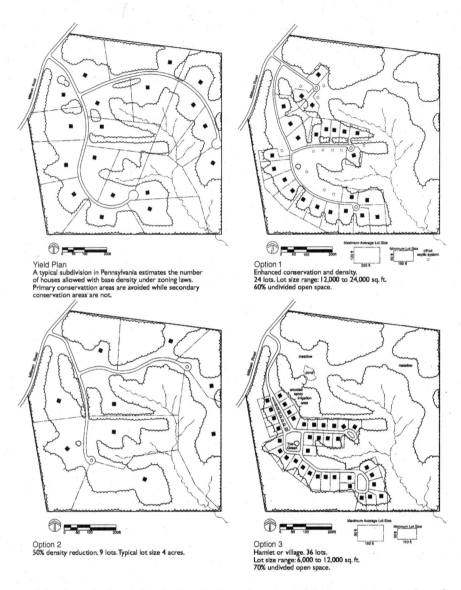

Yield Plan
A typical subdivision in Pennsylvania estimates the number of houses allowed with base density under zoning laws. Primary conservation areas are avoided while secondary conservation areas are not.

Option 1
Enhanced conservation and density.
24 lots. Lot size range: 12,000 to 24,000 sq. ft.
60% undivided open space.

Option 2
50% density reduction. 9 lots. Typical lot size 4 acres.

Option 3
Hamlet or village. 36 lots.
Lot size range: 6,000 to 12,000 sq. ft.
70% undivided open space.

A look at their method of analysis and at one of their projects has therefore been illustrated here.

Ringfield: Ring Road, Chadds Ford Township, Delaware County, Pennsylvania

CREDITS: Richard Chalfant (Developer)

HIGHLIGHT: Landscape infrastructure to treat water and purify soil and air

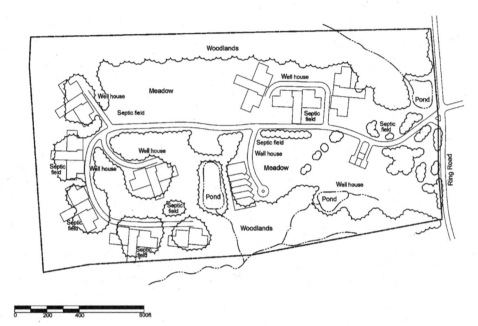

The rural development of Ringfield, Pennsylvania, clustered houses to preserve open meadows and wooded areas, while still maintaining residents' privacy. *Drawings by Natural Lands Trust, Inc. From Growing Greener by Randall Arendt. © 1999 Natural Lands Trust. Reprinted by permission of Island Press.*

A home at Ringfield, Pennsylvania, is integrated into forested natural areas and meadows. *Photo by Valerie Aymer, Natural Lands Trust, Inc.*

A project of 25 single-family detached houses, 2 semidetached ones, and 6 townhouses (varying from 2,700 to 3,600 square feet) were developed on a 64-acre site.

The significance of this project lies in the 55 of the 64 acres, which have been preserved as open meadows and woodlands. The houses occupy quarter-acre lots—no restrictions were placed on the developer as to lot size width or street frontage—and all the houses face front and back on permanent open space. The small lots seem, therefore, sufficiently spacious because they abut open space in the rear, and no land is wasted on front lawns. They have modest setbacks from the street, with dooryard gardens or informal landscaped areas. The original stone farmhouse on the land has been kept on an out-parcel. Homes are served by six deep wells. The six wells and the septic fields are all located in the common open space. Three constructed ponds provide for wildlife habitats and are used informally for ice skating in winter.

Widow's Walk Golf Course, Scituate, Massachusetts

CREDITS: Michael Hurdzan, Hurdzan-Fry Golf Course Design (Designer), International Golf Course Construction, Arlington, Massachusetts (Construction), International Golf Maintenance, Lakeland, Florida (Management)

HIGHLIGHT: A golf course built on abandoned gravel pits restores the environment

Golf courses are a special kind of land development: it creates relatively little impervious surface, but causes several other environmental impacts. Among these are release of potentially large quantities of fertilizers and pesticides, heavy water use, construction phase impacts, and habitat fragmentation. A typical 18-hole golf course can cover 100 or more acres, and there are more than 16,000 courses in the United States, so the aggregate effect can be great. Increasingly, golf courses seek to minimize their environmental impact through a variety of strategies, ranging from habitat protection and creation to organic greens care.

One of the most wide-ranging examples of environmentally sensitive golf course design is Widow's Walk in Scituate, Massachusetts. Described as an environmental demonstration golf course, Widow's Walk takes its name from the viewing cupolas located on the peaks of many local historical homes.

Almost every aspect of the course was designed to minimize environmental impacts. For starters, the course was built on an abandoned sand and gravel site, arguably a kind of brownfield. Abandoned in the 1970s, the property had become a site for illegal dumping, and was threatening a public water supply well in the sandy aquifer to which it drained.

Led by nationally recognized golf course designer Michael Hurdzan, a team of environmental experts was assembled to help design the course. The designer says this allowed the course to be built faster at lower cost, clearly important benefits for a developer. Sensitive habitat areas were identified and a links style course designed to avoid them. This goal could not be achieved with a completely continuous path through the site, so fully 7 of the 18 holes have "forced carries," gaps in fairways to protect especially vulnerable areas. Golfers must hit their shots over these "hazards" in order to advance their ball. This and the narrow fairways make for a challenging course, favored by many golfers. The design also was careful to leave a mix of habitat types, including wetlands, woods, vernal pools, vegetated streams, and open grasslands, among others. The diverse topography, partly a consequence of the sand and gravel operation, was allowed to remain, rather than being bulldozed.

The public water supply well is protected by buffer zones. In the immediate proximity of the well, no pesticide and fertilizer use are permitted. Farther away, but still in the well's watershed, reduced pesticide and fertilizer use are allowed. Much of the irrigation water for the course comes from another well, whose water quality falls below EPA drinking standards. This water infiltrates, is purified by natural soil processes, and resupplies the drinking well. In this way, much of the golf course functions as a large biofilter.

On other parts of the site, the goal is to use less than 50 percent of the fertilizer, pesticides, water, and fossil fuel of standard courses in the region. Among other things, this required planting drought-tolerant grasses and a willingness to tolerate occasional dry periods when fairway grasses were allowed to turn brown. Fairways are planted in creeping fescue, which can turn brown when water is scarce, but is drought-tolerant. Grass clippings are left on fairways to provide natural fertilizer, and pesticide use is minimized by following integrated pest management principles.

Greens are planted with a bentgrass hybrid developed for lower maintenance requirements. Clippings are removed, but are composted for later use. A wide variety of designs were used for the 18 greens' drainage, soil type, and soil amendments—the set comprises a kind of experiment. Instrumentation measures soil moisture, temperature, and fertility, and provisions were made to allow sampling the drainage to test its chemical composition. A number of researchers from universities and the private sector are using the course as a laboratory to understand nutrient flows, weed control, and other aspects of sustainable golf course management.

Widow's Walk in Scituate, Massachusetts, is an environmental demonstration golf course. It was built on a brownfield site and incorporates a broad range of environmental features ranging from carefully designed water-handling systems to restored and protected habitat. *Todd R. Hugill.*

The course has also been exemplary in terms of its use of recycled materials. Cart paths are constructed from crushed asphalt derived from repaving a nearby highway. Soil on the site, which was largely eliminated by the sand and gravel operation, was re-created using wood chips and sawdust from the site, along with pelletized sewage sludge from off-site to amend native sands. Perhaps the most novel form of recycling involved rug material that was illegally dumped at the site in the past. This was used to emulate sod walls to reinforce steep slopes on bunkers.

Habitat was not only protected, but plantings were carried out to increase the variety of food sources, and nesting boxes were installed. The Massachusetts Audubon Society, a partner in the enterprise, has identified 80 species of birds, some rare for the region.

Widow's Walk scores points in essentially every category of LAND Code recommendations, from site selection and water management to habitat protection and materials recycling. Importantly, despite its unconventional design, Widow's Walk has won numerous awards for its quality as a golf course, and golfers universally praise its aesthetic qualities and remarkable views. Built at a reasonable cost, avoiding neighbor opposition, and protecting and even enhancing the environment, Widow's Walk has been an example of win-win sustainable land development.

Sustainable Urbanism: Block Scale

Norddeutsche Landesbank am Friedrichswall, Hannover, Germany

CREDITS: Behnisch, Behnisch & Partner (now: Behnisch Architekten) (Architect), Wetzel + von Seht (Structural Engineer), Pfefferkorn + Partner (Structural Engineer), Ingenieurbüro Gierke (Mechanical Engineer), Nagel + Schonhoff (Landscape Architect)

HIGHLIGHT: Urban sustainability at the city-block scale

This project, which may seem the least landscape- or land-related, is a good example of what to do in a highly urbanized area where land is fully developed. Here, a central courtyard transfers clean air into the surrounding buildings, and a water feature used as a reflective surface serves to cool the courtyard by the water's evaporation. Instead of demolition, two existing buildings are folded into the overall new scheme.

Encompassing an entire city block, the Norddeutsche Landesbank in Hanover, Germany, incorporates existing buildings into its architecture and uses its large courtyard for bringing natural ventilation and fresh air into the offices. *Photo: Karl Joseph, 2006.*

This project is made to fit into Hannover's city grid. It takes up a whole block, lining the block's perimeter with six-story buildings, absorbing the two existing ones into this edge, and pushing the tall, new, modern office tower to the center of the block, which is made into a surrounding courtyard. As a result, the six-story perimeter buildings make the street frontage much more humane and urbane in this city-block-sized project. The main entrance, exhibition spaces, shops, and restaurants surround the courtyard and serve the streetscape on all four sides. The high-rise structure departs from the existing architecture and presents a volume of different heights and massing. It is an example of a very urban development with well-integrated, well-designed, and environmentally sound buildings.

The high-rise tower is set back, creating a more human-scaled presence on the street. The double façades protect the offices from noise and pollution and serve as a duct to bring in fresh air from the courtyard. *Javier Gonzalez-Campana.*

A large portion of the tower is naturally ventilated. Areas of "double façades" to the highly trafficked streets provide protection against noise and vehicle emissions in the six-story perimeter buildings. These "double façades," praised by some and doubted as to their ecological effectiveness by others, serve as a duct, transferring clean air from the central courtyard to the individual offices. The large area of water in the courtyard increases the reflection of daylight and creates a cool microclimate. Roof gardens act to improve the general climate for the occupants and to collect rainwater for irrigation and use within the building. Numerous terraces provide the staff with informal seating areas and new viewpoints over the city. Plants have been used as accent only, except for the roof plantings of the staff restaurant, which has a seasonally changing landscape. The reduced vegetation elsewhere is justified in terms of not wanting to make landscape an element of its own.

The whole complex is sustainable, on the one hand using a mix of strategies to fit the prevalent building types in Hannover, and on the other creating a new, modern, and environmentally sound tower. The tower is not an isolated element or overpowering street structure, but plays the role of a sculpture set back and seen at a distance. At the same time, its surrounding buildings maintain the traditional streetscape scale and treatment of Hannover.

Sustainable Urbanism: City Scale

The Photonics Center in Adlershof, Berlin, Germany

CREDITS: Sauerbruch Hutton Architects (Architect), Buro Schrickel (Landscape Architect), Zibell Willner & Partner (Environmental Engineering), Krebs & Kiefer GmbH (Structural Engineering), Ingenierburo Michael Lange (Façade Consultants)

HIGHLIGHT: Sustainability at city scale

The Center for Photonics and Optical Technology illustrates the large city-sized work of WISTA, a government-sponsored development and management agency, in Adlershof, a technology district in Berlin. The basic sustainable strategy for developing Adlershof has been to take a part of Berlin, which has a long technological history, and reuse most of the buildings on-site, while bringing in new buildings as infill. Part of that technological history includes buildings such as one from the early German aviation industry (Lilienthal), a center for research and production for Hitler's Luftwaffe; the television broadcasting company Deutscher Fernschfunk; and the Academy of Science, and the East German Security Service. All are being reused. In addition, part of Humboldt University (4,000 students, 800 professors) has been integrated into its research institutes. And during an annual science fair on the site, all the buildings are opened to the general public.

WISTA also chose a site with a superb transportation infrastructure: three airports close by, an interurban electric railway system, and streetcar and bus lines. In addition, bike paths and bike parking installations have been woven throughout the site. Eighty percent of the people arriving on-site are expected to come via public transportation or bikes. Car-share centers on-site are also part of the project.

Looking at one project in particular clarifies the strategy. The Photonics Center built two new buildings amid two older structures, to become part of the whole. The center offers subsidized rental space to photonics companies; two other building lots in the vicinity are also offered for lease or purchase. The site's water must be treated through a chain of ponds, through which water is cleaned before leaving the grounds. Permeable areas are mandatory on the side of all streets. They collect all the water traversing the site and empty it in a large reservoir on the side of the site called Stadt Park, which comprises 181 hectares, 66 of which is a public park. Most streets on the site are narrow and nonlinear, to reduce car speed.

Though its urbanism and its new-old strategy are what matter most, the new buildings of the Photonics Center have modern environmental features. The façade of the three-story building is double-skinned, which enables natural ventilation for the layer of offices at the perimeter, while also providing a thermal buffer. And to accommodate the large number of magnificent trees on the site, the architect divided the original plan in two. The buildings were completed in 1998, at the cost of 17.3 million deutschmarks, or about $11 million.

The two new buildings of the Photonics Center fit into the existing structure and function of the neighborhood but also stand out due to their modern curvilinear architecture. *Copyright 2002, WISTA Management GMBH.*

Swales catch and filter runoff from impervious surfaces throughout the Photonics Center site. *Javier Gonzalez-Campana.*

The mixing of new buildings with renovated old ones, the environmental characteristics of the new buildings and their surroundings, the very liberal leasing arrangements, the integration with Humboldt University, and the connection to public transportation combine to form a synergy of education, research, transportation (elevated railway), technology, and urbanism. The result is an example of another way to achieve environmental and sustainable goals.

Rio Piedras Stream Restoration, San Juan, Puerto Rico

CREDITS: Field Operations (Landscape Architect), Applied Ecological Services (Ecological Consultant), Marcello Garcia PhD (Engineering Consultant), Toro Ferrer Arquitectos (Architect)

Highlight: Storm management for a city

The existing botanical garden today is bounded by a flood-prone river and dense residential neighborhoods, and is halved by a six-lane thoroughfare. The north parcel is flat, underused, and inaccessible; the south parcel is hilly and encompasses the University Central Administration building and the original display gardens. *Field Operations with Toro Ferrer Arquitectos, Gabriel Berriz Associates, and Applied Ecological Services.*

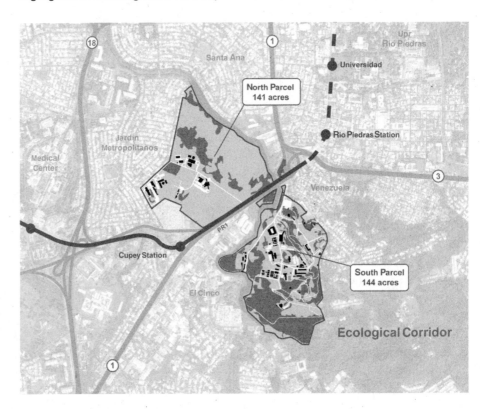

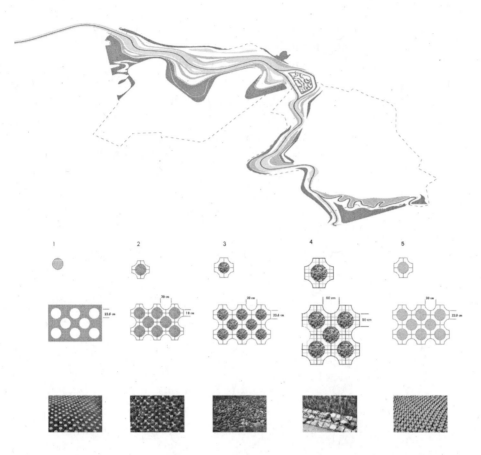

Floodways and bank stabilization techniques were studied in terms of their porosity aspect ratio, capacity to retain soil, and stability. *Field Operations with Toro Ferrer Arquitectos, Gabriel Berriz Associated, and Applied Ecological Services.*

This is a 250-acre site in the center of San Juan, the capital city of Puerto Rico. The Rio Piedras stream forms the boundary of one side, a section 1.5 miles long. Dense urban neighborhoods surround it on all other sides.

The Rio Piedras has many of the problems typical of urban streams: the watershed has been paved and built over, and the waters over the whole surface are drained to the stream, resulting in excessive flooding and high water speeds. The presence of the botanical garden used as a water management tool and an urban public amenity is the focus of this project. The U.S. Army Corps of Engineers had originally planned to guide the stream into a concrete channel, due to its proximity to residences and the unavailability of land to be purchased around the stream. But this went against the interest in keeping the river accessible to the public, an interest backed by the botanical garden and the Special Commission for the Ecological Capital of San Juan.

The solution proposed by Field Operations, with a team of hydrologists and ecologists, included, first, having the botanical garden allocate a portion of its land to allow for a new floodplain, which could slow down water and retain some of the overflow in basins.

The new design of the river consists of three shelves that vary in width and reinforcement techniques. They serve for overflow and public use. The low-flow channel, 10 meters (33 feet) wide, 1.5 meters (5 feet) minimum in depth, and lined with continuous riprap, will carry the daily flow. Narrow channels under bridges and close to buildings are also lined with riprap. It is a floodway shelf that provides for a typical two-to-ten–year recurrence interval, and is partly vegetated and partly lined with vegetated riprap. This flood-

Rio Piedras north shows submerged native plant exhibits and educational trails that traverse the shelves. *Field Operations with Toro Ferrer Arquitectos, Gabriel Berriz Associated, and Applied Ecological Services.*

way is primarily used for research, experimentation, and education. A secondary, higher shelf provides for 100-year floods. Its width depends on specific site locations and is used primarily for recreation. This shelf, because it is stressed less frequently, is reinforced with erosion control textiles and vegetation. The sloped embankments between shelves are vegetated revetment or riprap of varying thicknesses, depending on constraints and vegetation type.

Belmar, Lakewood, Colorado

CREDITS: Continuum Partners, LLC (Developer), Civitas, Inc., and EDAW (Urban Designers and Landscape Architects), Elkus/Manfredi Architects, Ltd., Van Meter Williams Pollack, Architecture Denver, and QPK Design (Architects)

HIGHLIGHT: Recycling of urban space

In the 1990s, many American cities witnessed the demise of the shopping center. In the case of the City of Lakewood in Colorado, it presented a redevelopment opportunity in a town in need of upgrading.

A 104-acre abandoned mall served to create a new city center in the old Villa Italia mall at Belmar. The new plan was the result of a partnership between Continuum Partners and the City of Lakewood. Continuum's parent company is the Pioneer Development Company of Syracuse. Continuum concentrates on sustainable buildings projects and community redevelopment opportunities in Colorado.

The partnership worked for a year on a plan for a new downtown. The city manager and city planner helped this first stage of public meetings, research, and ownership issues. The city bought the property and its buildings in 1999–2000. The city also stepped in with tax incentives to help the project along when Continuum had difficulties securing bank loans for a mixed-use project in a weak market.

The buildings on site were recycled: about 90 percent of the materials of the original buildings were reused. A public art project of wind turbines was used to produce enough energy for streetlights. Security personnel were put in Segway scooters instead of cars.

Construction for the first phase of the project began in 2002 and was completed in 2004. The remaining build-out is expected to take seven years. Total square feet figures allocate 1.2 million of retail space and 800,000 of office space, a hotel, and 1,300 residential units. Forty retail stores are under construction, as well as the largest Whole Foods store in the country.

An outdated shopping mall gives way to a mixed-use urban center, shown here in August 2005, with about a third of the project completed. At full build-out, the town of Lakewood, Colorado, will have a 22-block, pedestrian-friendly downtown area. *Courtesy of Continuum Partners, LLC.*

Belmar has diverse urban elements: a 2-acre park, a plaza, movie theaters, an ice skating rink, and cultural programs. The 1-acre plaza serves as the town's focal point, surrounded by residences and programmed for events throughout the summer. In winter, the plaza is turned into an ice skating rink. Houses vary from loft to urban rowhouses, live-work units, condominiums, and rentals.

The project's greatest contribution to sustainability comes from making an abandoned suburban site into something more urban—and with higher-intensity use than its original dynamic—by increasing density and the creating of a town center. One might say that it is making a small town out of suburbia.

Brownfields

Alumnae Valley Restoration Project at Wellesley College, Massachusetts

CREDITS: Michael Van Valkenburgh Associates, Inc. (Landscape Architect), Vanasse Hangen Brustlin, Inc. (Civil Engineer), Haley & Aldrich, Inc. (Geotechnical Engineer), Mack Scogin Merrill Elam Architects (Architect), Pine & Swallow Associates, Inc. (Soil Scientist), Prairie Restorations, Inc. (Meadow Consultant)

HIGHLIGHT: Conversion of a campus brownfield to better hydraulic function for stormwater treatment

A master plan for Wellesley College was started in 1997, and a 13.5-acre, 175-car parking lot was indicated as a potential area of new development for the campus. In spite of Frederick Law Olmsted, Jr., in 1902, urging the college to preserve the glacial topography and valley ecology, this parking lot area had historically been the site of natural-gas pumping and the college's physical plant. Consequently, toxic, contaminated soils lay beneath the asphalt pavement. The area that was to later become Alumnae Valley was a forgotten remnant of the college's initial development, which subsequently had experienced neglect and destruction of the original hydrological system and ecological function during the twentieth century.

A new campus building to be constructed north of the site would make the valley an increasingly important link between both the physical and experiential aspects of the campus, as well as an increasing pedestrian focus on campus.

The Van Valkenburgh firm proposed that radical changes be made to this valley in order to restore the historical function of the area as a watershed, address the toxicity of the soils on the site, and reconnect the area to its surrounding buildings.

The seven-year project involved transforming the use, topography, and soils of the site. A new parking garage was built to shift the parking burden to a more compact use near the new campus center. The removal of the old parking lot's asphalt required that highly contaminated soils be identified, removed, and treated off-site; less contaminated soils were dealt with in situ:

Remediation strategies were employed to both contain and remove toxic soils, as well as restore the biological integrity of the soil system. *Michael Van Valkenburgh Associates, Inc.*

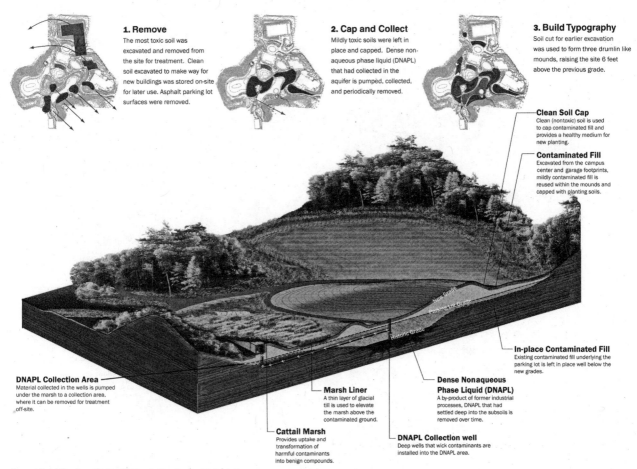

1. Remove
The most toxic soil was excavated and removed from the site for treatment. Clean soil excavated to make way for new buildings was stored on-site for later use. Asphalt parking lot surfaces were removed.

2. Cap and Collect
Mildly toxic soils were left in place and capped. Dense nonaqueous phase liquid (DNAPL) that had collected in the aquifer is pumped, collected, and periodically removed.

3. Build Typography
Soil cut for earlier excavation was used to form three drumlin like mounds, raising the site 6 feet above the previous grade.

Clean Soil Cap
Clean (nontoxic) soil is used to cap contaminated fill and provides a healthy medium for new planting.

Contaminated Fill
Excavated from the campus center and garage footprints, mildly contaminated fill is reused within the mounds and capped with planting soils.

In-place Contaminated Fill
Existing contaminated fill underlying the parking lot is left in place well below the new grades.

Dense Nonaqueous Phase Liquid (DNAPL)
A by-product of former industrial processes, DNAPL that had settled deep into the subsoils is removed over time.

DNAPL Collection well
Deep wells that wick contaminants are installed into the DNAPL area.

Marsh Liner
A thin layer of glacial till is used to elevate the marsh above the contaminated ground.

Cattail Marsh
Provides uptake and transformation of harmful contaminants into benign compounds.

DNAPL Collection Area
Material collected in the wells is pumped under the marsh to a collection area, where it can be removed for treatment off-site.

Brownfield Restoration—Efficiently Dealing with Toxicity
A variety of soil remediation techniques are used to treat the contaminated site and restore it as a living system.

they were turned into part of a new topography composed of three drumlin-like mounds, capped with clean fill, resulting in the entire site being raised 6 feet above its previous grade. Pumps were installed to regularly remove the toxic liquid by-products of the site's historic natural gas processing industry.

The valley's hydrological function as a connection to a larger 80-acre watershed was the major ecological focus of the site's design. A wetland was constructed within the new topography of the valley and incorporated into a system of holding and treating the site's water runoff, before flowing into Lake Waban. A series of rocky forebays capture runoff and allow sediments to settle out of the water before it flows into the wetland, whose clay lining seals off contaminated soils from reentering the hydrologic system. Cattails, forbs,

A new topography and plant community were put in place to store and treat surface water on the Alumnae Valley site.
Michael Van Valkenburgh Associates, Inc.

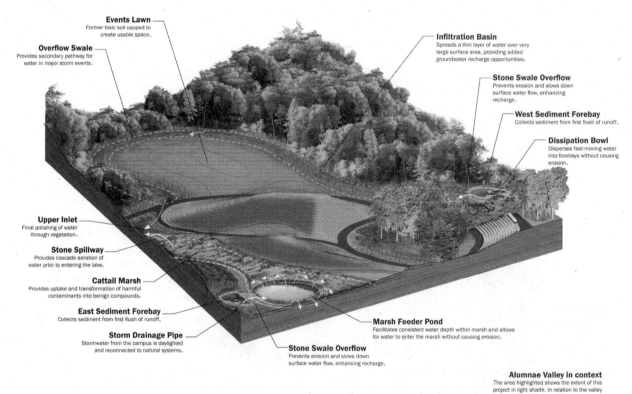

Events Lawn
Former toxic soil capped to create usable space.

Overflow Swale
Provides secondary pathway for water in major storm events.

Infiltration Basin
Spreads a thin layer of water over very large surface area, providing added groundwater recharge opportunities.

Stone Swale Overflow
Prevents erosion and slows down surface water flow, enhancing recharge.

West Sediment Forebay
Collects sediment from first flush of runoff.

Dissipation Bowl
Disperses fast-moving water into forebays without causing erosion.

Upper Inlet
Final polishing of water through vegetation.

Stone Spillway
Provides cascade aeration of water prior to entering the lake.

Cattail Marsh
Provides uptake and transformation of harmful contaminants into benign compounds.

East Sediment Forebay
Collects sediment from first flush of runoff.

Storm Drainage Pipe
Stormwater from the campus is daylighted and reconnected to natural systems.

Marsh Feeder Pond
Facilitates consistent water depth within marsh and allows for water to enter the marsh without causing erosion.

Stone Swale Overflow
Prevents erosion and slows down surface water flow, enhancing recharge.

Alumnae Valley in context
The area highlighted shows the extent of this project in light shade, in relation to the valley system of Wellesley's campus (in dark shade).

Reconnecting Systems—Using Topography and Hydrology to Treat Surface Water
Through ecological restoration techniques and hydrological design, Alumnae Valley is reinstated as part of the glacial topography and ecology that Olmsted cited as Wellesley's unique and valuable legacy.

The McCann parking lot before and after the Wellesley Alumnae Valley restoration project completion in 2004—what was an impermeable parking lot is now a wetland. *Top: MVVA. Bottom: Paul Warchol.*

and sedges in the wetland and pond help purify the runoff. The drumlin-shaped mounds are planted in native meadow species, and the site incorporates more than 300 planted native tree species.

This valley's restoration incorporates the landscape into the area's watershed by bringing back the site's hydrologic function, while simultaneously ameliorating the toxic legacy of the site's history.

Ford Rouge Motor Plant, Dearborn, Michigan

CREDITS: D.I.R.T. Studio (Environmental Engineering Consultant), Nelson Byrd Woltz Landscape Architects (Landscape Architect), Cahill Associates (Engineer), Dr. Clayton Rugh (Phytoremediation Scientist), William McDonough + Partners (Architect)

HIGHLIGHT: A landscape infrastructure

A number of factors make this a twenty-first century project in sustainability. These are the project's scale (1,200 acres); the intent of recycling a very important industrial plant of the twentieth century to make it one of the twenty-first century; and the use of green roofs, stormwater management, and phytoremediation as the first strategy for this transformation.

In 1999, the Ford Motor company announced its plan for a 20-year renovation of the Rouge River Manufacturing Plant and its intention to make it a symbol of sustainable manufacturing. New manufacturing plants are included in this plan, as well as a master plan for a sustainable landscape infrastructure for the whole site.

The stormwater management starts with a 10.4-acre green roof of sedum. Excess water from the roof drains into stone basins under an absorbent porous parking lot. The water then flows into a network of swales planted with native trees, shrubs, and grasses. The enormous grid of swales over the site is capable of retaining 90 percent of the annual rainfall. The swales and additional treatment wetlands serve as filters, sending cleaner water into the ground, rivers, and lakes.

Phytoremediation is the other sustainable strategy used, consisting of the removal of polluting materials through plants. Specifically in this case, PAH compounds (polyaromatic hydrocarbons), the highly carcinogenic by-products of steel manufacturing, are being removed from the soil around the coke ovens of the manufacturing plant.

Plants, or rather microbes on their roots, break down contaminants into harmless organic compounds, which are absorbed into the roots. With funding from Ford, two researchers, Clayton Rugh of Michigan State University and

Native shrubs, shown here immediately after planting, create a colorful mosaic while providing stormwater management and wildlife habitat. *D.I.R.T. Studio/Nelson Byrd Woltz Landscape Architects.*

John Thomas of the University of Michigan—Dearborn, developed a phyto-remediation system using native plants. The project is now in its fourth year.

The best performers were joe-pyeweed, New England aster, and leadplant. Phytoremediation on this site is showing 50 percent degradation in three to five years, at the very least. When compared to the alternative of removing the polluted soil to a landfill or letting it degrade on its own (which would take decades, perhaps a century), this is a dramatic and productive sustainable strategy for this site.

Methods and Materials

LivingHomes, LLC, Santa Monica, California

CREDITS: Steve Glenn (CEO and Founder), Ray Kappe, FAIA, and David Hertz, AIA (Architects)

HIGHLIGHT: Green prefabrication: a way to build that is less destructive of natural systems

This work-in-progress represents an effort to create modern sustainable pre-fabricated homes designed by good architects. Though prefabrication refers specifically to building activity, it is included here because it is much less

These prefabricated homes can be erected in a few hours, thereby having much less construction impact on the site. © 2006 LivingHomes, LLC. Tom Bonner—Photographer.

destructive of natural systems. Construction activity is very hard on a site: it disturbs drainage patterns; cuts down existing vegetation, not just for the footprint of the building, but also for a large surrounding area; and it brings the constant activity of trucks for materials delivery and the construction equipment itself. Typically, this activity goes on for a long period of time—one year to five years, depending on the size of project. In contrast, this project was erected in eight hours.

Prefabrication also saves considerable construction waste over traditional site-built methods (40 percent of construction material ends up in landfills versus 2 percent for prefab). Prefabrication has, however, had a checkered history, never quite living up to its promise of affordable or medium-priced housing. This new effort at prefabrication assembles environmental materials in a factory setting. The materials have all been vetted and chosen for their environmentally sustainable qualities. But there is also a series of partnerships with companies working in sustainable design: appliances by BOSCH, LED lighting by PermLight, photovoltaic cells by PermaCorp, fixtures by Kohler, Forest Stewardship Council-certified lumber by Eco-Lumber Co-op, special roofing by Carlysle, a spa by Jacuzzi, and furnishings by Design Within Reach.

The homes produce their own energy, use no city water for irrigation, and strive to eliminate waste and carbon emissions in production. © 2006 LivingHomes, LLC. Tom Bonner—Photographer.

The LivingHomes model home in Santa Monica, California, which is the first home to receive a LEED platinum rating from the U.S. Green Building Council, was designed by Ray Kappe, founder of Sci-Arch School of Architecture in Los Angeles. In April 2006, this model was installed—more accurately, lowered—onto a concrete slab in 11 modules by a 350-ton crane over the space of eight hours, an important reduction in site construction activity. From April to July 2006, when the house was finished, all the construction was mainly interior.

The home does not use city water for irrigation. Instead, a rooftop garden insulates the home, absorbs sunlight (reducing the heat island effect of standard black roofs), and features a stormwater management system that collects rainwater in a cistern to be used for landscaping irrigation. A graywater system collects and recycles water from the sink and shower for irrigation purposes.

Steve Glenn, the founder of LivingHomes, has three other houses on the way and is planning a whole development in Joshua Tree, California. The stated goal of the project is zero energy, zero water, zero waste, zero carbon, and zero emissions. LivingHomes buildings are described as nature-made and factory-built (versus stick-built). In the end, it may be sustainability that fulfills prefabrication's promise to the building industry.

GreenSkate Laboratory, Washington, DC

CREDITS: Terri Nostrand (Project Director), Chris Nostrand and Ben Ashworth (Construction Foremen), Andy Neal (Procurement and Communications), Jaime Stapula (Volunteer Coordinator), MSG, Bodar Masonry and Artisan Concrete Services (Concrete Experts), Luke Jouppi and Omer Windham (Design), Don Hawkins (Architectural Consultant)

HIGHLIGHT: Recycled materials

This facility built on an abandoned handball court to serve as a skate park is a useful example on more than one count. First, it shows how to recycle a sport facility to accommodate a currently popular sport. Second, it recycles a material that is very difficult to dispose of: used tractor-trailer tires, many of which were pulled up from the Anacostia River on cleanup days.

Using recycled materials and volunteer energy, the Green-Skate Laboratory is a model of green architecture, environmental education, and community building. *Jeff Perona, www.nagchaumpa.com.*

The idea for the project came out of experimental work done in the 1970s in the Southwest for building thick walls covered in adobe, which provide good insulation against heat and cold. Earthship Biotecture, Taos, New Mexico (www.earthship.org), is one of the present-day firms working with this method, which uses tires filled with earth. This technique is the one used by Ed Paschich with his Passage Construction Company in Corrales, New Mexico, which he founded in 1976. He is also the author of *The Tire House Book* (Sunstone Press, 1995*).*

Terri and Chris Nostrand—both skateboarders—put together a group of volunteer skateboarders who created a Play-Doh model of what they would like to see on the site. The Department of Parks and Recreation allowed them to convert the former handball court. The volunteers rammed earth into the tires and shaped the configuration of the skate park, putting earth and rebar on top of the tires. A group of skateboarders with experience in concrete poured the concrete on top, 6 inches thick, with rebar in it. Everything but the concrete was recycled, including the chain-link fence around the park and the coping on the concrete bowl (from a swimming pool). The volunteers acquired their knowledge about the tire and earth wall from the Internet.

Recycling materials from an urban sport facility and using volunteer skateboarders' time on weekends made for a different approach to creating a public facility, replacing the usual, top-down professional design. And though not imitable in that sense, it is an interesting case of the transmission of knowledge both in building and in recycling through the use of the Internet. This web-acquired know-how also points to the importance of creating accessible tools and examples of sustainability to demonstrate the basic science needed to both replicate and improve upon the project. This is also one of the aims of this book.

Industrial Ecology

Kalundborg Industrial Park, Kalundborg, Denmark

PARTNERS: ENERGI E2, Statoil, Novo Nordisk, Gyproc, Bioteknisk Jordrens, the Town of Kalundborg

HIGHLIGHT: Industrial symbiosis

This Danish industrial park, or rather "eco-industrial park," as it is usually listed, is, on the surface, just that. But it is cited repeatedly as the ideal model, not just of an industrial park, but of any city or commercial enterprise. The number of enterprises (six) it contains—an oil refinery, a power station, a plasterboard company, a soil remediation company, a biotechnology company, and the town of Kalundborg itself—is impressive. But the real attraction is that each of these entities benefits from, and is based on, the waste of the others, so that the issue of disposing of polluting waste is minimized and the reuse of the waste gives fuel to another entity. Thus, the project has emerged as a standard bearer for true sustainability. It is also mentioned as a model for planning new industries and towns.

What is most curious about this example is that it was not planned from above or from the outside, but that it was self-organized, starting in 1961, with a partnership between a new oil refinery and the city of Kalundborg. Other partnerships followed until this interchange of materials among partners gave rise to what is considered today to be *industrial ecology*.

Each new partner became the recipient of the material or energy of one of the enterprises already in existence, setting off a series of material/energy exchanges. Only some of those exchanges will be mentioned here and only among the six main partners: the Asnaes power station (the largest coal-fired plant in Denmark); Statoil, an oil refinery belonging to the Norwegian State oil company; Novo Nordisk, a multinational biotechnology company (the largest producer of insulin and industrial enzymes); Gyproc, a Swedish plasterboard company; Bioteknisk Jordrens, a soil remediation company; and the town of Kalundborg.

Water, a scarce resource in Denmark, is gathered from Lake Tissø, rather than from groundwater, for the power station and other enterprises. The Statoil refinery provides further assistance: it sends its purified wastewater, as well as its used cooling water, to the Asnaes power station. Asnaes in turn supplies steam to Statoil and Novo Nordisk, and they therefore function with these two sources of water. Asnaes added a desulfuration process from its flue gases, and the resulting gypsum serves as the raw material for making plasterboard at Gyproc, which used to have to import gypsum from Spain. Novo Nordisk's used biomass is recycled as a fertilizer, which is used by the local farming community. Residual heat is provided by Asnaes to the heating system for the town.

The park shows a dramatic reduction in the consumption of valuable resources, as well as a reduction in waste, and this has also saved money. All of

The formidable industrial exterior of the Kalundborg complex hides the remarkable sustainable practices going on inside. *Photo by Weslynne Ashton.*

these successes and savings have been well traced and monitored, and Kalundborg has become the symbol of industrial ecology and of a system that eliminates waste, puts it to work, and reduces costs of production. Yet even a glance at the image of this town and its industrial symbiosis cannot but cause a negative reaction to the physical lack of integration and the failure of a happy aesthetic resolution to the town/industry combination. It is a combination dominated by the oil refinery and its many oil tanks, which dominate the landscape. In other words, the symbiosis has worked ecologically, but it has still not been made to function aesthetically or socially.

Partnerships

The formation of public-private partnerships is a potential mechanism for financing green development projects. Public dollars can be obtained for development projects that provide public benefits. Partnerships between environmentally conscious nonprofit organizations can also aid in the financing of green development through "tax avoidance vehicles, donations, and infrastructure development" (Rocky Mountain Institute [RMI] 1998). Additional advantages include benefits in the form of preferred financing by lending institutions, expertise related to local and/or environmental matters, and increased public support of the development. Case studies of such partnerships are included here.

Beacon Landing, Beacon, New York

MAJOR PARTNERS: Scenic Hudson Inc. and Ned Foss, CGI & Partners

A partnership between Scenic Hudson Inc. (a nonprofit environmental organization), Ned Foss of CGI & Partners (a for-profit development group), and the City of Beacon, New York, enables 23 acres of waterfront land to be developed into an ecologically sound yet economically feasible green hotel, marina, and waterfront park. Scenic Hudson Inc.'s mission to "protect and enhance the scenic, natural, historic, agricultural, and recreational treasures of the Hudson River and its valley" has attracted Ned Foss's for-profit development group to satisfy their overlapping goals. Scenic Hudson Inc. owns the 23-acre site and signed a 99-year facilities management lease with the development group. In addition to stimulating Beacon's economic development, the partnership will yield city tax revenue and provide waterfront open space and river access to Beacon residents.

Approximately $30 million will be spent for land acquisition, environmental resource assessments, community planning, and construction of a 90-room hotel and incidental facilities, totaling 160,000 square feet of building on several levels with built space covering 2 acres (Linder 2003). The majority of site area will be parkland (Wolf 2002).

The fact that the Beacon Landing site plans are being coordinated and endorsed by Scenic Hudson Inc. reduces the City of Beacon's fear of "greenwashing" by the developer. Enhanced local public support and reduced opposition to the green developer have set the table for a groundbreaking environmentally responsive project. Scenic Hudson invested significantly on the front end of the process before the developer was selected. They assembled the site, held it, and voluntarily left the property on the tax rolls. Thus, the developer's purchase and holding costs were eliminated.

Waterfront development of Beacon Landing as a former industrial site next to the city center and an adjacent New York City commuter rail station has created a domino redevelopment effect; specifically, it has attracted the Dia Center for the Arts and the Rivers and Estuaries Center on the Hudson. Beacon was selected in spring 2003 to be the site of the Rivers and Estuaries Center on the Hudson, a world-class scientific research and education institution expected eventually to have a $50 million annual operating budget. These attractions are expected to draw thousands of visitors annually (Polgreen 2003). Moreover, Beacon Landing is stimulating the City of Beacon's economic development, attracting downtown housing revitalization and raising property values. This steadily improving regional economic climate further enhances the potential economic benefits for the town and Beacon Landing.

Because Scenic Hudson has the prestige to obtain public funds for environmental projects, solar energy systems and waterfront redevelopment proposals for Beacon Landing receive hundreds of thousands of dollars from New York State energy and environmental protection grants (Office of the Governor of NY 2003). The developer, too, benefits from the cost savings generated by grant money, which further enhances the green project's likelihood of financial success. Some initial site planning and all site remediation have been paid for by Scenic Hudson Inc. All subsequent community-based reviews will be paid for by the developer. The developer accrues cost and time savings because less capital is used for site study.

However, if Scenic Hudson wanted a "must be green" clause in the lease to ensure that the project will be operated in a green manner, a mortgage would be difficult to obtain, as there are no objective standards of "green operation." Therefore, the developer would have to proceed in consultation with the local community, which can slow the process. The developer would lose some profit from the imposition of a lower-density project by Scenic Hudson, compared to what was allowable by zoning. However, the profitability of the hotel market for the region could cover the lower-density profit tradeoff. Green development has long-term profitability and, as a result, the payback of the green investment is sometimes slower than other types of investment under current market conditions.

The Civano Project, Tucson, Arizona

MAJOR PARTNERS: Case Enterprises, Trust for Sustainable Development (Initial Partner), City of Tucson, Arizona

The Civano Project, a 916-acre "sustainable urban village" in Tucson, Arizona, was initially a partnership between Case Enterprises and the Trust for Sustainable Development based in British Columbia. Ultimately, Case Enterprises bought out the trust's shares of the project and formed a partnership with the City of Tucson for risk sharing and some financial support. This partnership alleviated some of the developer's concerns, primarily that building conservation-oriented structures would "price themselves out" of Tucson's sprawling suburban market by directing growth to specific locations (RMI 1998).

The city will spend approximately $2.3 million for land, $30 million for site development, and $400 million for construction costs, of which $38 million will be financed through municipal bonds issued by the city for infrastructure. The city will also spend $4 million in future general obligation bonds for parks and recreation and an additional $3 million for other infrastructure improvements (RMI 1998).

The City of Tucson, as a financial and political partner of the project, is able to reduce high future infrastructure costs of sprawling development, saving $500,000 annually, while "proactively direct[ing] growth into high-density, clustered development in areas where growth is already occurring" (RMI 1998). The developer does not need to spend time convincing lending institutions of the benefits of compact development, as the city is a major lending partner. The project also benefits from a low interest rate on tax-exempt financing. Additionally, up to 10 percent of the Civano Project's profits will be placed into a fund for sustainability research on Tucson and the region (RMI 1998). This research could enhance the region's efficient use of resources, providing additional infrastructure and energy savings for the city.

The city's $7 million infrastructure and community center investments require political and financial support from taxpayers, but are expected to be repaid within eight years. Civano homes are expected to sell for a $10,000 premium, which tenants will partially recover through special tax assessments spread over 25 years, as well as life-cycle operation savings.

Builders for the Bay, Chesapeake Bay, Maryland

MAJOR PARTNERS: National Association of Home Builders (NAHB), Center for Watershed Protection (CWP), Chesapeake Bay Alliance (CBA)

Builders for the Bay is a partnership of the National Association of Home Builders (NAHB), the Center for Watershed Protection (CWP), and the Chesapeake Bay Alliance (CBA) that promotes environmentally responsible residential and commercial site development for the rapidly growing population of the Chesapeake Bay watershed. The partnership brings local homebuilders together with environmentalists to ensure environmentally responsible site development at the local level. It enables development and environment interests to create jointly supported development code reforms for a local municipality. This consensus provides communities with the support needed to enact local-level changes to promote sound environmental and economic development.

The administrative costs of convening partners and producing model development principles for local municipalities are nominal.

This common-ground approach significantly reduces the costs of lobbying and litigation for both environment and development groups and enables community needs to become more of a focus of the development process. Jointly supported recommendations provide significant time savings for the developer, thanks to minimal environmental and community opposition. The upfront participation of the NAHB has made local building associations more willing to participate. Ultimately, this consensus development with community support will minimize the longer-term environmental damages to the Chesapeake Bay fishery, water quality, and recreation opportunities.

Consensus building does, however, require more upfront time spent by developers and environmental groups, is an economic hurdle for the partnerships, and incurs the costs of partnership roundtables and document preparation.

Points Checklist

DIRECTIONS: For columns (b) and (c), fill in each box with 1 (yes) or 0 (no). In column (d), multiply point value in column (a) by column (b), then sum column (d) to get maxiumum achievable points for your site. In column (e), multiply point value in column (a) by column (c), then sum column (e) to get total points achieved for your site. The ratio of (e)/(d) determines the LAND certification level, either silver (40–60%), gold (60–80%), or platinum (80–100%). Enter a single value in any boxes that link two rows.

	(a) Point value	(b) All sites	Large sites	Parking on site	Streets on site	Buildings on site	Special site conditions	(c) Recommendation implemented	(d) (a) x (b)	(e) (a) x (c)
Site Drainage										
Design a drainage plan.	Req									
Model hydrology.	Req									
Map site's hydrologic features.	Req									
Implement drainage plan with swales, rain gardens, check dams, and so on.	12	1							12	
Preserve contour.	12	1							12	
Immediately stabilize new drainage structures with vegetation.	5	1							5	
Impervious Surfaces										
Use or emulate < 10 percent impervious cover.	10	1							10	
Limit street widths to 22 feet.	5									
Optimize street network to limit length.	6									
Site design includes cul-de-sacs.	-4									
Use smart cul-de-sac design (small diameter or center vegetated island).	3									
Place parking below buildings.	7				x					
Include parking spaces for compact vehicles and carpools.	4									
Limit parking spaces.	6									
Use pervious paving materials for all low-traffic areas, including driveways.	8	1							8	
Leave 15 percent of parking areas as rain gardens.	7									
Isolate imperviousness to patches.	5	1							5	
Install green roofs.	10									
Stormwater Quality										
Use mulching mowers and leave clippings, or use yard waste compost as fertilizer.	3	1							3	
Install catch basin inserts for advanced treatment.	4									
Clean out catch basins when 50 percent full.	4									

Points Checklist (Continued)

DIRECTIONS: For columns (b) and (c), fill in each box with 1 (yes) or 0 (no). In column (d), multiply point value in column (a) by column (b), then sum column (d) to get maximum achievable points for your site. In column (e), multiply point value in column (a) by column (c), then sum column (e) to get total points achieved for your site. The ratio of (e)/(d) determines the LAND certification level, either silver (40–60%), gold (60–80%), or platinum (80–100%). Enter a single value in any boxes that link two rows.

	(a) Point value	(b) All sites	(b) Large sites	(b) Parking on site	(b) Streets on site	(b) Buildings on site	(b) Special site conditions	(c) Recommendation implemented	(d) (a) x (b)	(e) (a) x (c)
Stormwater Quality (Continued)										
Use alternative to NaCl for parking lot/road salting.	2									
Provide dog waste bag dispensers.	2									
Septic systems on site.										
Maintain septic systems at least every 2 years.	3									
Polish septic effluent (aerobic unit, sand filter, treatment wall).	4									
Treat stored water from 5-year storm if not reused or infiltrated on site.	5	1							5	
Construct wetlands for stormwater treatment.	7									
Water Conservation and Reuse										
Redirect runoff during storms to water lawns and gardens.	5	1							5	
Use native or noninvasive plants that do not require irrigation beyond natural rainfall amount.	4	1							4	
Capture up to 5-year recurrence or 24-hour stormflow and reuse or time release.	10	1							10	
Erosion Prevention and Control										
Map site: slopes, buildings, disturbed soils, and flow paths.	Req									
Prepare erosion control plan.	Req									
Monitor turbidity in downslope streams.	Req									
Inspect and maintain erosion controls after every storm or at least every seven days.	Req									
Phase construction to minimize simultaneous soil disturbance.	9	1							9	
Clear only building footprint and minimal construction envelope.	12	1							12	
Site includes riparian zone.										
Leave vegetation in > 15 m riparian zone during construction.	5									
Install erosion control measures before soil disturbance.	8	1							8	

Points Checklist (Continued)

DIRECTIONS: For columns (b) and (c), fill in each box with 1 (yes) or 0 (no). In column (d), multiply point value in column (a) by column (b), then sum column (d) to get maxiumum achievable points for your site. In column (e), multiply point value in column (a) by column (c), then sum column (e) to get total points achieved for your site. The ratio of (e)/(d) determines the LAND certification level, either silver (40–60%), gold (60–80%), or platinum (80–100%). Enter a single value in any boxes that link two rows.

	(a) Point value	(b) All sites	(b) Large sites	(b) Parking on site	(b) Streets on site	(b) Buildings on site	(b) Special site conditions	(c) Recommendation implemented	(d) (a) x (b)	(e) (a) x (c)
Erosion Prevention and Control (Continued)										
Development of sites with slopes over 7 percent.	-6									
On cleared slopes over 7 percent (4 degrees), protect same day with blanket, mulch, turf, hydroseed, and so on.	5									
Development of sites with slopes over 17 percent.	-6									
Do not clear slopes over 17 percent (10 degrees).	5									
Schedule construction to match growing season.	4	1							4	
Soil Health and Integrity										
Remove and stockpile topsoil and replace after construction.	6	1							6	
Avoid compaction to maintain soil hydraulic conductivity.	6	1							6	
Aerate compacted soils to restore structure and hydraulic conductivity.	5	1							5	
Air Quality and Microclimate										
Prepare dust control plan.	Req									
Wet or rapidly stabilize disturbed soils.	3	1							3	
Inventory mature trees on the site.	5	1							5	
Retain all mature trees except those on building footprint and minimal construction envelope.	10	1							10	
Plant native or naturalized (noninvasive) trees after construction.	7	1							7	
Plant deciduous trees to south of buildings.	2					☐				
Plant native or naturalized (noninvasive) trees in parking lot rain gardens.	7			☐						
Determine wind rose for summer and winter conditions.	2	1							2	
Plant evergreens to block prevailing wind direction in winter.	2					☐				
Leave open pathway for prevailing wind direction in summer.	2						☐			

Points Checklist (Continued)

DIRECTIONS: For columns (b) and (c), fill in each box with 1 (yes) or 0 (no). In column (d), multiply point value in column (a) by column (b), then sum column (d) to get maxiumum achievable points for your site. In column (e), multiply point value in column (a) by column (c), then sum column (e) to get total points achieved for your site. The ratio of (e)/(d) determines the LAND certification level, either silver (40–60%), gold (60–80%), or platinum (80–100%). Enter a single value in any boxes that link two rows.

	(a) Point value	(b) All sites	Large sites	Parking on site	Streets on site	Buildings on site	Special site conditions	(c) Recommendation implemented	(d) (a) x (b)	(e) (a) x (c)
Preserving and Restoring Habitat										
Living resources conservation plan.	Req									
Development site is a brownfield.	25									
Development site previously developed, but not a brownfield.	12									
Development of sites with ecologically sensitive areas.	-10									
Do not disturb ecologically sensitive areas (steep slopes, ridgelines, and floodplains).	9									
Leave 70 percent of site undisturbed with existing native vegetation.	15									
Leave 50 percent of site undisturbed with existing native vegetation.	10									
Site has degraded habitat.										
Restore 20 percent of damaged land to functioning habitat.	10									
Use cluster development to leave open space.	10									
Buffering Critical Habitats										
Development of site with wetlands, streams, lakes, or seashores.	-25									
Leave an undeveloped buffer of 50 m around wetlands, streams, lakes, seashores, and nature preserves.	20									
Leave an undeveloped buffer of 30 m around wetlands, streams, lakes, seashores, and nature preserves.	10									
Development of sites with vernal pools.	-20									
Leave an undeveloped buffer of 100 m around vernal pools.	15									
Site's roads cross streams.	-8									
Stream crossings by roads should be designed to minimize environmental impact.	6									
Landscape Connectivity										
Provide 50 m-wide corridor across site connecting to habitat or corridor.	20									
Provide 30 m-wide corridor across site connecting to habitat or corridor.	10									

Points Checklist (Continued)

DIRECTIONS: For columns (b) and (c), fill in each box with 1 (yes) or 0 (no). In column (d), multiply point value in column (a) by column (b), then sum column (d) to get maxiumum achievable points for your site. In column (e), multiply point value in column (a) by column (c), then sum column (e) to get total points achieved for your site. The ratio of (e)/(d) determines the LAND certification level, either silver (40–60%), gold (60–80%), or platinum (80–100%). Enter a single value in any boxes that link two rows.

	(a) Point value	(b) All sites	Large sites	Parking on site	Streets on site	Buildings on site	Special site conditions	(c) Recommendation implemented	(d) (a) x (b)	(e) (a) x (c)
Road Placement and Design										
Provide migration passages under roads.	5									
Optimize street network to limit length (see "Impervious Surfaces" above).	0									
Limit residential roads to 22-ft width (see "Impervious Surfaces" above).	0									
Native Species and Landscape Heterogeneity										
Use 100 percent native or naturalized (noninvasive) plants.	7	1							7	
Preserve natural landscape heterogeneity.	6	1							6	
Maintain spatial and age structure of undeveloped areas.	3									
Invasive species present on site.										
Eradicate invasive species.	7									
Site requires pest control.										
Use Integrated Pest Management.	6									
Energy										
Public transit available in region.										
Locate within 1/2 mile of public transit.	6									
Locate within 1 mile of public transit.	3									
Provide shuttle to public transit.	4									
Provide dedicated parking for carpool and high-mileage vehicles.	4									
Provide bike racks.	2									
Generate renewable energy on site.	12	1							12	
Use only full cutoff light fixtures.	5	1							5	
Industrial Ecology and Materials										
Significant excavation of on-site material.	-12									
Reuse excavated material on-site for fill.	10									

Points Checklist (Continued)	(a)	(b)						(c)	(d)	(e)
DIRECTIONS: For columns (b) and (c), fill in each box with 1 (yes) or 0 (no). In column (d), multiply point value in column (a) by column (b), then sum column (d) to get maxiumum achievable points for your site. In column (e), multiply point value in column (a) by column (c), then sum column (e) to get total points achieved for your site. The ratio of (e)/(d) determines the LAND certification level, either silver (40–60%), gold (60–80%), or platinum (80–100%). Enter a single value in any boxes that link two rows.	Point value	All sites	Large sites	Parking on site	Streets on site	Buildings on site	Special site conditions	Recommendation implemented	(a) x (b)	(a) x (c)
Industrial Ecology and Materials *(Continued)*										
Use recycled concrete and asphalt for paving materials or fill.	3									
Compost or chip removed brush and trees for on-site reuse.	4	1							4	
Use recycled crumb rubber for paved pedestrian paths.	3									
Require packaging takeback by suppliers (e.g., pallets, containers, and shrink wrap).	3	1							3	
Make construction waste and unused materials available for reuse by others.	3	1							3	
Limit discards to 10 percent of construction materials delivered to site.	5	1							5	
Purchase construction materials from sources within 100 miles of site (shipped by truck, or 300 miles if shipped by rail).	4	1							4	
								TOTAL		
								(e)/(d)		

Glossary

absorption: Uptake of a substance from solution by a solid material, such as soil particles. In this book, we use the term broadly, whether technically adsorption (uptake onto a surface) or absorption (uptake into a solid) is actually meant.

baseflow: The amount of water flowing in streams or channels between storm events. Imperviousness causes elevated stormflows and depressed baseflows.

best management practices (BMPs): Structures or activities that help protect the environment. A more straightforward name might be *environmental management practices*, but BMP is a widely used term of art.

biochemical oxygen demand (BOD): The amount of oxygen consumed by a volume of water as a consequence of the presence of biodegradable organic matter. Sewage is one kind of contaminant that contributes high BOD to water.

biodiversity: The variability among living organisms, including diversity within species (genetic diversity), between species (species diversity), and of ecosystems (richness of ecosystem processes and interactions). In common usage, it often means, simply, the number of species in a location.

bioengineered structures: Structures made of natural materials, such as fiber mats, or constructed land forms, such as grass-lined depressions.

biome: A major regional collection of plant and animal communities adapted to the region's physical environment, terrain, altitude, and latitude.

bioretention areas: Sloped surfaces or depressions covered with soil and vegetation that slow and absorb rainwater runoff, filtering out pollutants. Same as a *rain garden*.

blackwater: Water from flushed toilets and chemical intensive sources, such as dishwashers and sinks with garbage disposals. Requires substantial treatment before disposal or most reuses. Compare to *graywater*.

brownfield: The U.S. Environmental Protection Agency (EPA) defines a brown-field site as property, the expansion, redevelopment, or reuse of which may be complicated by the presence or potential presence of a hazardous substance, pollutant, or contaminant. Compare to *greenfield*.

catchment: See *watershed*.

channel storage capacity: The volume of a stream network within its banks.

closed-loop recycling: The concept of reusing materials after their original purpose is fulfilled, effectively ending the need to dispose of discarded materials in a landfill, where they are wasted. The concept models itself on nutrient and other cycles in nature where material is continually recycled and not wasted.

cluster development: Buildings concentrated in one part of a site to reduce infrastructure and costs while maximizing connected areas of open space.

constructed wetland: A wetland built to replicate the processes occurring in natural marshlands, especially slowing runoff to reduce stormflow and filtering out pollutants to improve water quality. Two major types exist. *Free surface-constructed wetlands* have ponded water, while *subsurface flow constructed wetlands* are wet and marshy, but have standing surface water only under the wettest conditions.

contaminant: A substance found in air, water, or soil at levels higher than would occur naturally. Compare to *pollutant*.

cradle-to-grave: A type of material or product assessment that considers impacts at each stage of a product's life cycle, from the time natural resources are extracted and processed through each subsequent stage of manufacturing, transportation, product use, and disposal.

design for environment (DFE): Use of industrial ecological concepts to design products, with the aim of closing the loop on materials waste.

detention/retention ponds: Constructed ponds for temporary storage of excess stormwater built to prevent flooding or erosion. The temporary storage allows time for sediments and the pollutants they carry to settle out.

dissolved oxygen: The amount of oxygen dissolved in a given amount of water. In general, higher dissolved oxygen levels in lakes and streams indicate better ecosystem conditions. Lowered oxygen levels can harm aquatic life, and can be caused, for example, by runoff from hot pavement, unshaded streams, or the presence of sewage or too much fertilizer.

drainage basin: See *watershed*.

effective imperviousness: The amount of impervious surface that connects directly to off-site water conveyances or natural channels. Equivalent to total imperviousness, less isolated patches, surfaces draining to rain gardens, surfaces draining to vegetated soils, and the like.

embodied (or embedded) energy: The sum of the energy necessary to produce a service or product, including energy used in raw material extraction, transport, manufacturing, assembly, and installation.

endangered species: Any species that is in danger of extinction throughout all or a significant portion of its range.

energy flows: Within industrial ecology (IE), a term for the transfer of energy from one state to another. With reference to the IE of development projects, it is an assessment of the amount of energy used to extract, process, transport, and dispose of the products and materials that are used by the project.

eutrophication: Increase in productivity of a stream or lake, with consequent changes in algal communities, lowering of oxygen levels, and potential fish kills. *Accelerated or cultural eutrophication* is the result of excess levels of nitrogen and phosphorus in lakes, rivers, streams, and estuaries, caused by fertilizer, sewage systems, animal manure, pet waste, and other sources. Also called *nutrient pollution.* Technically, *eutrophication* is the natural evolution of water bodies, whereas *cultural eutrophication* is the acceleration of these processes caused by added nutrients.

evapotranspiration (ET): The total amount of water vapor released to the atmosphere by physical evaporation from land and water surfaces, along with water vapor returned to the atmosphere by plants through their natural metabolic processes.

fascines: Fascines are long, rope-like bundles of branches or twigs, generally tied together in some fashion.

first flush: The phenomenon whereby the maximum in contaminant concentration occurs during storms before the greatest flow.

flow regimes: The seasonal pattern or variation in the amount and speed of water flowing in streams or rivers.

graywater: Water from sources such as the bath, shower, washing machine, bathroom sink, and kitchen sink (in the absence of a dishwasher or garbage disposal). Graywater has intermediate quality between potable water and blackwater. It requires little or slight treatment before disposal, and is usually directly suitable for purposes such as irrigation. Compare to *blackwater.*

greenfield: A parcel of land not previously developed beyond agricultural or forestry use; virgin land. Compare to *brownfield.*

green roofs: Gardens or vegetation installed over normal roofing material that collect rainwater and reduce water runoff and insulate buildings, especially in urban environments.

greenwashing: Giving a positive public image to environmentally unsound practices.

hydrologic: Pertaining to the movement of water.

hydrology: The study of the occurrence, properties, and movement of water on and beneath the surface of the earth.

hydroseed: A mixture of grass seeds, mulch, fertilizer, bonding agents, and water. Hydroseed is sprayed on the land surface, stabilizes the surface against erosion, and germinates more rapidly than grass seed alone.

impervious cover: Land surface, such as conventional street pavement or highly compacted soil, that does not allow water to pass through it to the subsurface. Compare to *effective imperviousness*.

industrial ecology (IE): A systems approach, evaluating the interaction of industrial and natural systems and the flows of materials and energy through those systems. The aim is to increase materials use efficiency and reduce the impact of materials use with the goal of closing the loop of materials cycling.

industrial symbiosis: A relationship between industrial facilities where they benefit from exchanging materials created from each other's manufacturing processes. For example, gypsum can be created as a by-product of power generation and is discarded from this activity, but can be used as an input for manufacturing plasterboard. *Symbiosis* is a biological relationship in which at least two otherwise unrelated species exchange materials, energy, or other resources.

infiltration: The process of precipitation passing below the earth's surface; that portion of water.

integrated pest management (IPM): A system of controlling pests that aims to use up-to-date knowledge and varied strategies to minimize risk to people and harm to the environment. It does not preclude use of synthetic pesticides, but rather minimizes their use by drawing on a variety of strategies based on knowledge of the life histories of pests. It also takes advantage of the intrinsic properties of various pesticides, such as their degradation rate, solubility, and specificity.

life-cycle assessment (LCA): Quantifying the environmental impacts of a product, process, or activity, examining the whole cycle from extraction of resources through to recycling or disposal. LCA includes assessment of the flow of energy and water and discards to air and water, as well as solid emissions resulting from the product life cycle.

low-impact development (LID): Also, *low-impact design*. A system of designing hydrologic systems distributed across the landscape to simulate natural water movement, minimize stormflows, and protect water quality.

materials flow: Within industrial ecology, pathways of materials used to create any product, from a book to a development site. Materials are tracked from their extraction or manufacture to their use in the product through their disposal when discarded.

National Pollutant Discharge Elimination System (NPDES): A regulatory program under the Clean Water Act that prohibits the discharge of pollutants into U.S. surface waters without a permit.

nephelometric turbidity unit (NTU): The standard unit when testing turbidity with a nephelometer, a meter that works by measuring the amount of light scattered by suspended sediment. As a rule of thumb, 1 NTU corresponds to about 1 mg/L (milligram per liter) of suspended sediment.

nonpoint source pollution (NPS): Pollution caused by contaminant sources that are distributed across the landscape. NPS contrasts with point sources, such as sewage and industrial wastes, which usually enter the environment from large individual discharges. Two of the main nonpoint sources are urban and agricultural land uses.

nutrient pollution: The negative effects of excess levels of nitrogen and phosphorus in lakes, rivers, and streams resulting from fertilizer, sewage systems, animal manure, pet waste, and other sources. Also called *eutrophication*.

pervious cover: Land surface, such as grass, forest, or loose soil, that allows water to pass into it to the subsurface.

PM2.5, PM10: Airborne particulate matter (dust) with average effective particle size of less than or equal to 2.5 μm (micrometer) and 10 μm, respectively. A micrometer (μm) is one millionth of a meter, or about 1/25,000 of an inch. Human hair ranges in thickness from 40 to 100 micrometers.

pollutant: A contaminant causing harm to an ecosystem. Compare to *contaminant*.

potable: Suitable for drinking.

rain garden: Vegetated depression into which runoff is diverted and where infiltration to groundwater and evapotranspiration can occur. Same as a *bioretention area*.

receiving water: A stream, river, lake, estuary, or ocean into which contaminated water flows.

recurrence interval: Average frequency with which a storm of a given magnitude recurs. For example, a 5-year storm will happen, on average, 20 times each century. However, two 5-year storms could occur in a single year or 20 years apart; it is the long-term average recurrence that matters. Recurrence interval is applied to storms of specific lengths, typically 3 hours, 6 hours, 12 hours, and 24 hours.

residence time: The average amount of time that a molecule of water remains in a given lake, pond, or stream or in each part of the earth's water cycle (e.g., in the atmosphere, on the earth's surface, or in groundwater).

riparian zone: The area immediately adjacent to a river or stream, though sometimes extended to include a lake or estuary. There is no universally accepted width of this zone.

runoff: The portion of precipitation that reaches streams. Contrast with *evapotranspiration*.

soil hydraulic conductivity: The capacity of a soil to convey water.

storm event: A rain- or snowstorm delivering measurable precipitation to a site.

stormflow: The elevated flow of water in streams and channels during and immediately after storms.

storm hydrograph: A graphical representation of the changes in flow that occur during a storm. A typical storm hydrograph shows a rapid rise to peak stormflow followed by a gradual decline and return to baseflow.

stormwater: Water that flows off the land surface during and just after storms and that contributes to stormflow. Stormwater typically carries elevated levels of contaminants.

subwatershed: A smaller watershed nested within a larger one. The term is relative, as any watershed can be broken into smaller pieces, and all but the largest basins combine to form even bigger ones. See also *watershed*.

suspended sediment: Particulate matter carried by moving water. Water running across the land surface or eroding stream channels picks up particles of soil, silt, and sand. Swift water can carry more sediment than slow-moving water. Excessive amounts of suspended sediment caused by erosion can be harmful to aquatic systems by blocking sunlight to submerged plants, choking filter-feeding animals, and burying bottom-dwelling organisms as water slows down and deposits on stream or lake bottoms. Small particles of sediment often carry toxic pollutants, such as heavy metals and pesticides, and these pollutants can degrade water quality.

swales: Shallow, constructed, linear, earthen depressions designed to slow down and temporarily store excess rainwater during or just after storms, to prevent flooding and allow time for rainwater to be absorbed into the ground. *Vegetated swales* are lined with grass or other vegetation to help filter out pollutants and to reduce erosion.

threatened species: A species that is likely to become an endangered species within the foreseeable future throughout all or a significant portion of its range.

Total Maximum Daily Load (TDML): A program under the Clean Water Act designed to help control diffuse sources of pollution, such as urbanization and other land development.

turbidity: A surrogate measurement of the amount of suspended particles in a volume of water, based on the amount of light that is scattered by particles in the water. In common terms, it is the "cloudiness" of the water.

vegetated swales: See *swales*.

watershed: The area of land contributing water as runoff or subsurface drainage to a point. Usually, people are interested in the watershed of locations along the length of a stream. However, every point has a contributing watershed. Watersheds are easily delineated from topographic maps and are separated from each other by drainage divides, ridges that can be subtle or dramatic. Watershed boundaries are objectively defined. A simpleminded example of a watershed is a bathtub, which forms the watershed of its drain; and a roof is the watershed of its downspout. Other terms that are used more or less synonymously with watershed are *drainage basin* and *catchment*, though the former is usually applied to large watersheds and the latter to small ones.

References

CHAPTER 2: WATER

Ahmed, W., R. Neller, and M. Katouli. 2005. Host species-specific metabolic fingerprint database for enterococci and Escherichia coli and its application to identify sources of fecal contamination in surface waters. *Applied and Environmental Microbiology* 71 (8):4461–4468.

Amweg, E. L., D. P. Weston, J. You, and M. J. Lydy. 2006. Pyrethroid insecticides and sediment toxicity in urban creeks from California and Tennessee. *Environmental Science & Technology* 40 (5):1700–1706.

Bay Area Stormwater Management Agencies Association. 1999. Start at the Source—Design Guidance Manual for Stormwater Quality Protection.

Berndtsson, J. C., T. Emilsson, and L. Bengtsson. 2006. The influence of extensive vegetated roofs on runoff water quality. *Science of the Total Environment* 355 (1–3):48–63.

Bomboi, M. T., and A. Hernandez. 1991. Hydrocarbons in urban runoff: Their contribution to the wastewaters. *Water Research* 25 (5):557–565.

Booth, D. B., and C. R. Jackson. 1997. Urbanization of aquatic systems: Degradation thresholds, stormwater detection, and the limits of mitigation. *J. Amer. Water Resour. Assoc.* 33 (5):1077–1090.

Brabec, E., S. Schulte, and P. L. Richards. 2002. Impervious surfaces and water quality: A review of current literature and its implications for watershed planning. *Journal of Planning Literature* 16 (4):499–514.

Brown, T. S. 1987. Household hazardous-waste—the unresolved water-quality dilemma. *Journal Water Pollution Control Federation* 59 (3):120–124.

Burnes, B. S. 2003. Antibiotic resistance analysis of fecal coliforms to determine fecal pollution sources in a mixed-use watershed. *Environmental Monitoring and Assessment* 85 (1):87–98.

Carpenter, S. R., N. F. Caraco, D. L. Correll, R. W. Howarth, A. N. Sharpley, and V. H. Smith. 1998. Nonpoint pollution of surface waters with phosphorus and nitrogen. *Ecological Applications* 8 (3):559–568.

Castro, M. S., C. T. Driscoll, T. E. Jordan, W. G. Reay, and W. R. Boynton. 2003. Sources of nitrogen to estuaries in the United States. *Estuaries* 26 (3):803–814.

Center for Watershed Protection. 2003. Impacts of Impervious Cover on Aquatic Systems. Ellicott City, MD.

Chang, M. T., M. W. McBroom, and R. S. Beasley. 2004. Roofing as a source of nonpoint water pollution. *Journal of Environmental Management* 73 (4):307–315.

Christensen, E. R., A. Li, I. A. AbRazak, P. Rachdawong, and J. F. Karls. 1997. Sources of polycyclic aromatic hydrocarbons in sediments of the Kinnickinnic River, Wisconsin. *Journal of Great Lakes Research* 23 (1):61–73.

Coulter, C. B., R. K. Kolka, and J. A. Thompson. 2004. Water quality in agricultural, urban, and mixed land use watersheds. *Journal of the American Water Resources Association* 40 (6):1593–1601.

Councell, T. B., K. U. Duckenfield, E. R. Landa, and E. Callender. 2004. Tire-wear particles as a source of zinc to the environment. *Environmental Science & Technology* 38 (15):4206–4214.

Djokic, D., and D. R. Maidment. 1993. Application of GIS network routines for water-flow and transport. *J. Water Resour. Planning. Management—ASCE* 119 (2):229–245.

Dougherty, M., R. L. Dymond, T. J. Grizzard, A. N. Godrej, C. E. Zipper, and J. Randolph. 2006. Quantifying long-term NPS pollutant flux in an urbanizing watershed. *Journal of Environmental Engineering—ASCE* 132 (4):547–554.

Dussaillant, A. R., C. H. Wu, and K. W. Potter. 2004. Richards equation model of a rain garden. *J. Hydrologic Engineer.* 9 (3):219–225.

Elvidge, C. D., C. Milesi, J. B. Dietz, B. T. Tuttle, P. C. Sutton, R. Nemani, and J. E. Vogelmann. 2004. U.S. constructed area approaches the size of Ohio. *Eos* 85 (24):233–234.

Faucette, L. B., C. F. Jordan, L. M. Risse, M. Cabrera, D. C. Coleman, and L. T. West. 2005. Evaluation of stormwater from compost and conventional erosion control practices in construction activities. *Journal of Soil and Water Conservation* 60 (6):288–297.

Geldreich, E. E. 1996. Pathogenic agents in freshwater resources. *Hydrological Processes* 10 (2):315–333.

Groffman, P. M., N. L. Law, K. T. Belt, L. E. Band, and G. T. Fisher. 2004. Nitrogen fluxes and retention in urban watershed ecosystems. *Ecosystems* 7 (4):393–403.

Jackson, R. B., and E. G. Jobbagy. 2005. From icy roads to salty streams. *Proc. Nat. Acad. Sci.* 102:14487–14488.

Janeau, J. L., A. Mauchamp, and G. Tarin. 1999. The soil surface characteristics of vegetation stripes in Northern Mexico and their influences on the system hydrodynamics—An experimental approach. *Catena* 37 (1–2):165–173.

Jones, J. E., T. A. Earles, E. A. Fassman, E. E. Herricks, B. Urbonas, and J. K. Clary. 2005. Urban storm-water regulations—Are impervious area limits a good idea? *J. Environ. Engineering—ASCE* 131 (2):176–179.

Kochel, R.C., J.R. Miller, M. Lord, and T. Martin. 2005. Geomorphic problems with in-stream structures using natural channel design strategy for stream restoration projects in North Carolina. Paper read at Geol. Soc. Amer. Annual Meeting, at Salt Lake City, UT.

Laws, E.A. 1993. *Aquatic Pollution.* 2nd ed. New York: John Wiley & Sons.

Line, D. E., J. A. Arnold, G. D. Jennings, and J. Wu. 1996. Water quality of stormwater runoff from ten industrial sites. *Water Resources Bulletin* 32 (4):807–816.

Line, D. E., N. M. White, D. L. Osmond, G. D. Jennings, and C. B. Mojonnier. 2002. Pollutant export from various land uses in the upper Neuse River Basin. *Water Environment Research* 74 (1):100–108.

Maidment, D. R. 1993. *Handbook of Hydrology.* New York: McGraw-Hill, Inc.

Makepeace, D. K., D. W. Smith, and S. J. Stanley. 1995. Urban stormwater quality—Summary of contaminant data. *Critical Reviews in Environmental Science and Technology* 25 (2):93–139.

Moore, A. A., and M. A. Palmer. 2005. Invertebrate biodiversity in agricultural and urban headwater streams: Implications for conservation and management. *Ecological Applications* 15 (4):1169–1177.

Ohe, T., T. Watanabe, and K. Wakabayashi. 2004. Mutagens in surface waters: a review. *Mutation Research-Reviews in Mutation Research* 567 (2–3):109–149.

Paul, M. J., and J. L. Meyer. 2001. Streams in the urban landscape. *Ann. Rev. Ecology Systematics* 32:333–365.

Petersen, T. M., H. S. Rifai, M. P. Suarez, and A. R. Stein. 2005. Bacteria loads from point and nonpoint sources in an urban watershed. *Journal of Environmental Engineering—ASCE* 131 (10):1414–1425.

Prestes, E. C., V. E. dos Anjos, F. F. Sodre, and M. T. Grassi. 2006. Copper, lead and cadmium loads and behavior in urban stormwater runoff in Curitiba, Brazil. *Journal of the Brazilian Chemical Society* 17 (1):53–60.

Prince George's County MD Department of Environmental Resources. 1999. Low-Impact Development Design Strategies—An Integrated Design Approach: Environmental Protection Agency.

Rice, K. C., K. M. Conko, and G. M. Hornberger. 2002. Anthropogenic sources of arsenic and copper to sediments in a suburban lake, northern Virginia. *Environmental Science & Technology* 36 (23):4962–4967.

Schiff, K., and M. Sutula. 2004. Organophosphorus pesticides in storm-water runoff from southern California (USA). *Environmental Toxicology and Chemistry* 23 (8):1815–1821.

Shinya, M., T. Tsuchinaga, M. Kitano, Y. Yamada, and M. Ishikawa. 2000. Characterization of heavy metals and polycyclic aromatic hydrocarbons in urban highway runoff. *Water Science and Technology* 42 (7–8):201–208.

Shirasuna, H., T. Fukushima, K. Matsushige, A. Imai, and N. Ozaki. 2006. Runoff and loads of nutrients and heavy metals from an urbanized area. *Water Science and Technology* 53 (2):203–213.

Sutherland, R. A., F. M. G. Tack, C. A. Tolosa, and M. G. Verloo. 2001. Metal extraction from road sediment using different strength reagents: Impact on anthropogenic contaminant signals. *Environmental Monitoring and Assessment* 71 (3):221–242.

Taebi, A., and R. L. Droste. 2004. Pollution loads in urban runoff and sanitary wastewater. *Science of the Total Environment* 327 (1–3):175–184.

Technical Release 55: Urban Hydrology for Small Watersheds. U.S. Department of Agriculture.

Wernick, B. G., K. E. Cook, and H. Schreier. 1998. Land use and streamwater nitrate-N dynamics in an urban-rural fringe watershed. *Journal of the American Water Resources Association* 34 (3):639–650.

Wong, N. H., S. F. Tay, R. Wong, C. L. Ong, and A. Sia. 2003. Life cycle cost analysis of rooftop gardens in Singapore. *Building and Environment* 38 (3):499–509.

CHAPTER 3: SOILS

Barrett, M. E., J. F. Malina, and R. J. Charbeneau. 1998. An evaluation of geotextiles for temporary sediment control. *Water Environment Research* 70 (3):283–290.

Coulter, C. B., R. K. Kolka, and J. A. Thompson. 2004. Water quality in agricultural, urban, and mixed land use watersheds. *Journal of the American Water Resources Association* 40 (6):1593–1601.

Demars, K. R., R. P. Long, and J. R. Ives. 2004. Erosion control using wood waste materials. *Compost Science & Utilization* 12 (1):35–47.

Dougherty, M., R. L. Dymond, T. J. Grizzard, A. N. Godrej, C. E. Zipper, and J. Randolph. 2006. Quantifying long-term NPS pollutant flux in an urbanizing watershed. *Journal of Environmental Engineering—ASCE* 132 (4):547–554.

Faucette, L. B., C. F. Jordan, L. M. Risse, M. Cabrera, D. C. Coleman, and L. T.

West. 2005. Evaluation of stormwater from compost and conventional erosion control practices in construction activities. *Journal of Soil and Water Conservation* 60 (6):288–297.

Harbor, J. 1999. Engineering geomorphology at the cutting edge of land disturbance: erosion and sediment control on construction sites. *Geomorphology* 31 (1–4):247–263.

Harbor, J. M., J. Synder, and J. Storer. 1995. Reducing nonpoint source pollution from construction sites using rapid seeding and mulching. *Physical Geography* 16 (5):371–388.

Herzog, M., J. Harbor, K. McClintock, J. Law, and K. Bennett. 2000. Are green lots worth more than brown lots? An economic incentive control on residential developments. *Journal of Soil and Water Conservation* 55 (1):43–49.

Kaufman, M. M. 2000. Erosion control at construction sites: The science-policy gap. *Environmental Management* 26 (1):89–97.

Kaufman, M. M., D. L. Wigston, and E. B. Perlman. 2002. Environmental evaluation of subdivision site developments. *Environmental Management* 29 (6):801–812.

Line, D. E., N. M. White, D. L. Osmond, G. D. Jennings, and C. B. Mojonnier. 2002. Pollutant export from various land uses in the upper Neuse River Basin. *Water Environment Research* 74:100–108.

Prince George's County MD Department of Environmental Resources. 1999. Low-Impact Development Design Strategies—An Integrated Design Approach: Environmental Protection Agency.

Science and Education Administration. 1978. Predicting Rainfall Erosion Losses: USDA.

Soupir, M. L., S. Mostaghimi, A. Masters, K. A. Flahive, D. H. Vaughan, A. Mendez, and P. W. McClellan. 2004. Effectiveness of polyacrylamide (PAM) in improving runoff water quality from construction sites. *Journal of the American Water Resources Association* 40 (1):53–66.

Tyler, R. 2001. Compost filter berms and blankets take on the silt fence. *Biocycle* 42 (1):26–31.

CHAPTER 4: AIR QUALITY AND MICROCLIMATE

Beckett, K. P., P. H. Freer-Smith, and G. Taylor. 2000. Particulate pollution capture by urban trees: effect of species and windspeed. *Global Change Biology* 6 (8):995–1003.

Brunekreef, B., and B. Forsberg. 2005. Epidemiological evidence of effects of coarse airborne particles on health. *European Respiratory Journal* 26 (2):309–318.

Ca, V. T., T. Asaeda, and E. M. Abu. 1998. Reductions in air conditioning energy caused by a nearby park. *Energy and Buildings* 29 (1):83–92.

Chow, J. C., J. G. Watson, M. C. Green, D. H. Lowenthal, D. W. DuBois, S. D. Kohl, R. T. Egami, J. Gillies, C. F. Rogers, C. A. Frazier, and W. Cates. 1999. Middle- and neighborhood-scale variations of PM10 source contributions in Las Vegas, Nevada. *Journal of the Air & Waste Management Association* 49 (6):641–654.

Delfino, R. J., C. Sioutas, and S. Malik. 2005. Potential role of ultrafine particles in associations between airborne particle mass and cardiovascular health. *Environmental Health Perspectives* 113 (8):934–946.

Dombrow, J., M. Rodriguez, and C. F. Sirmans. 2000. The market value of mature trees in single-family housing markets. *The Appraisal Journal* 68:39–43.

Fang, C. F., and D. L. Ling. 2003. Investigation of the noise reduction provided by tree belts. *Landscape and Urban Planning* 63 (4):187–195.

Guenther, A. 1997. Seasonal and spatial variations in natural volatile organic compound emissions. *Ecological Applications* 7 (1):34–45.

Kuo, F. E., and W. C. Sullivan. 2001. Environment and crime in the inner city—Does vegetation reduce crime? *Environment and Behavior* 33 (3):343–367.

McPherson, E. G. 1994. Energy-Savings Potential of Trees in Chicago. Gen. Tech. Report NE-186. In *Chicago's Urban Forest Ecosystem: Results of the Chicago Urban Forest Climate Project*, edited by E. G. McPherson, D. J. Nowak and R. A. Rowntree. Radnor, PA: U.S.D.A., Forest Service, Northeastern Forest Expt. Sta.

Nowak, D. J. 1994. Air pollution removal by Chicago's urban forest. Gen. Tech. Report NE-186. In *Chicago's Urban Forest Ecosystem: Results of the Chicago Urban Forest Climate Project*, edited by E. G. McPherson, D. J. Nowak and R. A. Rowntree. Radnor, PA: U.S.D.A., Forest Service, Northeastern Forest Expt. Sta.

Nowak, D. J., and D. E. Crane. 2002. Carbon storage and sequestration by urban trees in the USA. *Environmental Pollution* 116 (3):381–389.

Nowak, D. J., K. L. Civerolo, S. T. Rao, G. Sistla, C. J. Luley, and D. E. Crane. 2000. A modeling study of the impact of urban trees on ozone. *Atmospheric Environment* 34 (10):1601–1613.

Robitu, M., M. Musy, C. Inard, and D. Groleau. 2006. Modeling the influence of vegetation and water pond on urban microclimate. *Solar Energy* 80 (4):435–447.

Simpson, J. R. 2002. Improved estimates of tree-shade effects on residential energy use. *Energy and Buildings* 34 (10):1067–1076.

Smardon, R. C. 1988. Perception and aesthetics of the urban environment—Review of the role of vegetation. *Landscape and Urban Planning* 15 (1–2):85–106.

Stamps, A. E. 1997. Some streets of San Francisco: Preference effects of trees, cars, wires, and buildings. *Environment and Planning B-Planning & Design* 24 (1):81–93.

Stathopoulos, T., D. Chiovitti, and L. Dodaro. 1994. Wind shielding effects of trees on low buildings. *Building and Environment* 29 (2):141–150.

Van Renterghem, T., and D. Botteldooren. 2002. Effect of a row of trees behind noise barriers in wind. *Acta Acustica United with Acustica* 88 (6):869–878.

Vardoulakis, S., B. E. A. Fisher, K. Pericleous, and N. Gonzalez-Flesca. 2003. Modelling air quality in street canyons: a review. *Atmospheric Environment* 37 (2):155–182.

Xia, J. Y., and D. Y. C. Leung. 2001. Pollutant dispersion in urban street canopies. *Atmospheric Environment* 35 (11):2033–2043.

CHAPTER 5: LIVING RESOURCES

Andren, H. 1994. Effects of habitat fragmentation on birds and mammals in landscapes with different proportions of suitable habitat—A review. *Oikos* 71 (3):355–366.

Barton, A. M., L. B. Brewster, A. N. Cox, and N. K. Prentiss. 2004. Nonindigenous woody invasive plants in a rural New England town. *Biological Invasions* 6 (2):205–211.

Biggs, J., S. Sherwood, S. Michalak, L. Hansen, and C. Bare. 2004. Animal-related vehicle accidents at the Los Alamos National Laboratory, New Mexico. *Southwestern Naturalist* 49 (3):384–394.

Bodie, J. R. 2001. Stream and riparian management for freshwater turtles. *Journal of Environmental Management* 62 (4):443–455.

Brigham, D. 2001. Invasive shrubs and vines. *Landscape Architecture* 91 (11):24–+.

Bulger, J. B., N. J. Scott, and R. B. Seymour. 2003. Terrestrial activity and conservation of adult California red-legged frogs Rana aurora draytonii in coastal forests and grasslands. *Biological Conservation* 110 (1):85–95.

Burrell, C. C. 2001. Specifying native plants—Exercise caution in sourcing plants and seeds. *Landscape Architecture* 91 (3):22–+.

Carey, A. B., and C. A. Harrington. 2001. Small mammals in young forests: implications for management for sustainability. *Forest Ecology and Management* 154 (1–2):289–309.

Carr, L. W., and L. Fahrig. 2001. Effect of road traffic on two amphibian species of differing vagility. *Conservation Biology* 15 (4):1071–1078.

Chen, J. Q., J. F. Franklin, and T. A. Spies. 1995. Growing-season microclimatic gradients from clear-cut edges into old-growth Douglas-Fir forests. *Ecological Applications* 5 (1):74–86.

Clevenger, A. P., B. Chruszcz, and K. Gunson. 2001. Drainage culverts as habitat linkages and factors affecting passage by mammals. *Journal of Applied Ecology* 38 (6):1340–1349.

Clevenger, A. P., and N. Waltho. 2000. Factors influencing the effectiveness of wildlife underpasses in Banff National Park, Alberta, Canada. *Conservation Biology* 14 (1):47–56.

Conover, M. R., W. C. Pitt, K. K. Kessler, T. J. Dubow, and W. A. Sanborn. 1995. Review of human injuries, illnesses, and economic losses caused by wildlife in the United States. *Wildlife Society Bulletin* 23 (3):407–414.

Davies-Colley, R. J., G. W. Payne, and M. van Elswijk. 2000. Microclimate gradients across a forest edge. *New Zealand Journal of Ecology* 24 (2):111–121.

Debinski, D. M., and R. D. Holt. 2000. A survey and overview of habitat fragmentation experiments. *Conservation Biology* 14 (2):342–355.

deMaynadier, P. G., and M. L. Hunter. 2000. Road effects on amphibian movements in a forested landscape. *Natural Areas Journal* 20 (1):56–65.

Desbonnet, A., V. Lee, P. Pogue, D. Reis, J. Boyd, J. Willis, and M. Imperial. 1995. Development of coastal vegetated buffer programs. *Coastal Management* 23 (2):91–109.

Dodd, C. K., and B. S. Cade. 1998. Movement patterns and the conservation of amphibians breeding in small, temporary wetlands. *Conservation Biology* 12 (2):331–339.

Dramstad, W. E., J. D. Olson, and R. T. T. Forman. 1996. *Landscape ecology principles in landscape architecture and land-use planning.* Washington, DC: Island Press.

Fahrig, L. 2001. How much habitat is enough? *Biological Conservation* 100 (1):65–74.

Fahrig, L., J. H. Pedlar, S. E. Pope, P. D. Taylor, and J. F. Wegner. 1995. Effect of road traffic on amphibian density. *Biological Conservation* 73 (3):177–182.

Fennessy, M. S., and J. K. Cronk. 1997. The effectiveness and restoration potential of riparian ecotones for the management of nonpoint source pollution, particularly nitrate. *Critical Reviews in Environmental Science and Technology* 27 (4):285–317.

Forman, R. T. T., and L. E. Alexander. 1998. Roads and their major ecological effects. *Ann. Rev. Ecology Systematics* 29:207–+.

Gehlhausen, S. M., M. W. Schwartz, and C. K. Augspurger. 2000. Vegetation and microclimatic edge effects in two mixed-mesophytic forest fragments. *Plant Ecology* 147 (1):21–35.

Gurnell, A. M., K. J. Gregory, and G. E. Petts. 1995. The role of coarse woody debris in forest aquatic habitats—Implications for management. *Aquatic Conservation-Marine and Freshwater Ecosystems* 5 (2):143–166.

Hayward, G. D., P. H. Hayward, and E. O. Garton. 1993. Ecology of boreal owls in the northern Rocky Mountains, USA. *Wildlife Monographs* (124):1–59.

Henderson, S., T. P. Dawson, and R. J. Whittaker. 2006. Progress in invasive plants research. *Progress in Physical Geography* 30 (1):25–46.

Hickey, M. B. C., and B. Doran. 2004. A review of the efficiency of buffer strips for the maintenance and enhancement of riparian ecosystems. *Water Quality Research Journal of Canada* 39 (3):311–317.

Hobden, D. W., G. E. Laughton, and K. E. Morgan. 2004. Green space borders— a tangible benefit? Evidence from four neighbourhoods in Surrey, British Columbia, 1980–2001. *Land Use Policy* 21 (2):129–138.

Hodges, M. F., and D. G. Krementz. 1996. Neotropical migratory breeding bird communities in riparian forests of different widths along the Altamaha River, Georgia. *Wilson Bulletin* 108 (3):496–506.

Jansen, K. P., A. P. Summers, and P. R. Delis. 2001. Spadefoot toads (Scaphiopus holbrookii holbrookii) in an urban landscape: Effects of nonnatural substrates on burrowing in adults and juveniles. *Journal of Herpetology* 35 (1):141–145.

Jehle, R. 2000. The terrestrial summer habitat of radio-tracked great crested newts (Triturus cristatus) and marbled newts (T-marmoratus). *Herpetological Journal* 10 (4):137–142.

Joyal, L. A., M. McCollough, and M. L. Hunter. 2001. Landscape ecology approaches to wetland species conservation: a case study of two turtle species in southern Maine. *Conservation Biology* 15 (6):1755–1762.

Kogan, M. 1998. Integrated pest management: Historical perspectives and contemporary developments. *Annual Review of Entomology* 43:243–270.

Lamb, R. J., and A. T. Purcell. 1990. Perception of naturalness in landscape and its relationship to vegetation structure. *Landscape and Urban Planning* 19 (4):333–352.

Laurance, S. G., and W. F. Laurance. 1999. Tropical wildlife corridors: use of linear rainforest remnants by arboreal mammals. *Biological Conservation* 91 (2–3):231–239.

Laurance, W. F., L. V. Ferreira, J. M. Rankin-De Merona, and S. G. Laurance. 1998. Rain forest fragmentation and the dynamics of Amazonian tree communities. *Ecology* 79 (6):2032–2040.

Laurance, W. F., T. E. Lovejoy, H. L. Vasconcelos, E. M. Bruna, R. K. Didham, P. C. Stouffer, C. Gascon, R. O. Bierregaard, S. G. Laurance, and E. Sampaio. 2002. Ecosystem decay of Amazonian forest fragments: A 22-year investigation. *Conservation Biology* 16 (3):605–618.

Lehmkuhl, J. F., K. D. Kistler, and J. S. Begley. 2006. Bushy-tailed woodrat abundance in dry forests of eastern Washington. *Journal of Mammalogy* 87 (2):371–379.

McCoy, E. D., and H. R. Mushinsky. 1999. Habitat fragmentation and the abundances of vertebrates in the Florida scrub. *Ecology* 80 (8):2526–2538.

McKinney, M. L. 2002. Urbanization, biodiversity, and conservation. *Bioscience* 52 (10):883–890.

Mech, S. G., and J. G. Hallett. 2001. Evaluating the effectiveness of corridors: a genetic approach. *Conservation Biology* 15 (2):467–474.

Mesquita, R. C. G., P. Delamonica, and W. F. Laurance. 1999. Effect of surrounding vegetation on edge-related tree mortality in Amazonian forest fragments. *Biological Conservation* 91 (2–3):129–134.

Moore, A. A., and M. A. Palmer. 2005. Invertebrate biodiversity in agricultural and urban headwater streams: Implications for conservation and management. *Ecological Applications* 15 (4):1169–1177.

Naiman, R. J., H. Decamps, and M. Pollock. 1993. The role of riparian corridors in maintaining regional biodiversity. *Ecological Applications* 3 (2):209–212.

Nicholls, S., and J. L. Crompton. 2005. The impact of greenways on property values: Evidence from Austin, Texas. *Journal of Leisure Research* 37 (3):321–341.

Ozguner, H., and A. D. Kendle. 2006. Public attitudes towards naturalistic versus designed landscapes in the city of Sheffield (UK). *Landscape and Urban Planning* 74 (2):139–157.

Preisser, E. L., J. Y. Kefer, and J. D. Lawrence. 2000. Vernal pool conservation in Connecticut: An assessment and recommendations. *Environmental Management* 26 (5):503–513.

Prieur-Richard, A. H., and S. Lavorel. 2000. Invasions: the perspective of diverse plant communities. *Austral Ecology* 25 (1):1–7.

Primack, R. B. 2002. Overexploitation, Invasive Species, and Disease. In *Essentials of Conservation Biology*. Sunderland, MA: Sinauer Associates.

———. 2002. Problems of small populations. In *Essentials of Conservation Biology*. Sunderland, MA: Sinauer Associates.

Rheault, H., P. Drapeau, Y. Bergeron, and P. A. Esseen. 2003. Edge effects on epiphytic lichens in managed black spruce forests of eastern North America. *Canadian Journal of Forest Research-Revue Canadienne De Recherche Forestiere* 33 (1):23–32.

Richter, S. C., J. E. Young, R. A. Seigel, and G. N. Johnson. 2001. Postbreeding movements of the dark gopher frog, Rana sevosa goin and netting: Implications for conservation and management. *Journal of Herpetology* 35 (2):316–321.

Ricketts, T. H. 2001. The matrix matters: Effective isolation in fragmented landscapes. *American Naturalist* 158 (1):87–99.

Ricklefs, R. E. 1977. Environmental heterogeneity and plant species diversity—Hypothesis. *American Naturalist* 111 (978):376–381.

Savard, J. P. L., P. Clergeau, and G. Mennechez. 2000. Biodiversity concepts and urban ecosystems. *Landscape and Urban Planning* 48 (3–4):131–142.

Schueler, T. R. 1995. Chap. 5: The architecture for stream buffers. In *Site Planning for Urban Stream Protection*: Center for Watershed Protection.

Semlitsch, R. D. 2000. Principles for management of aquatic-breeding amphibians. *Journal of Wildlife Management* 64 (3):615–631.

Semlitsch, R. D., and J. R. Bodie. 1998. Are small, isolated wetlands expendable? *Conservation Biology* 12 (5):1129–1133.

Sieving, K. E., M. F. Willson, and T. L. De Santo. 2000. Defining corridor functions for endemic birds in fragmented south-temperate rainforest. *Conservation Biology* 14 (4):1120–1132.

Trombulak, S. C., and C. A. Frissell. 2000. Review of ecological effects of roads on terrestrial and aquatic communities. *Conservation Biology.* 14 (1):18–30.

van den Berg, A. E., C. A. J. Vlek, and J. F. Coeterier. 1998. Group differences in the aesthetic evaluation of nature development plans: A multilevel approach. *Journal of Environmental Psychology* 18 (2):141–157.

Wiktander, U., O. Olsson, and S. G. Nilsson. 2001. Seasonal variation in home-range size, and habitat area requirement of the lesser spotted woodpecker (Dendrocopos minor) in southern Sweden. *Biological Conservation* 100 (3):387–395.

Wilcove, D. S., D. Rothstein, J. Dubow, A. Phillips, and E. Losos. 1998. Quantifying threats to imperiled species in the United States. *Bioscience* 48 (8):607–615.

Young, A., and N. Mitchell. 1994. Microclimate and vegetation edge effects in a fragmented podocarp roadleaf forest in New Zealand. *Biological Conservation* 67 (1):63–72.

CHAPTER 6: ENERGY

Armstrong, R. J., and D. A. Rodriguez. 2006. An evaluation of the accessibility benefits of commuter rail in Eastern Massachusetts using spatial hedonic price functions. *Transportation* 33 (1):21–43.

Gibbons, S., and S. Machin. 2005. Valuing rail access using transport innovations. *Journal of Urban Economics* 57 (1):148–169.

McMillen, D. P., and J. McDonald. 2004. Reaction of house prices to a new rapid transit line: Chicago's midway line, 1983–1999. *Real Estate Economics* 32 (3):463–486.

CHAPTER 7: INDUSTRIAL ECOLOGY AND MATERIALS

Begum, R. A., C. Siwar, J. J. Pereira, and A. H. Jaafar. 2006. A benefit-cost analysis on the economic feasibility of construction waste minimisation: The case of Malaysia. *Resources Conservation and Recycling* 48 (1):86–98.

Duran, X., H. Lenihan, and B. O'Regan. 2006. A model for assessing the economic viability of construction and demolition waste recycling—the case of Ireland. *Resources Conservation and Recycling* 46 (3):302–320.

CHAPTER 8: ENVIRONMENTAL ENGINEERING

Barrett, M. E., J. F. Malina, and R. J. Charbeneau. 1998. An evaluation of geotextiles for temporary sediment control. *Water Environment Research* 70 (3):283–290.

Benik, S. R., B. N. Wilson, D. D. Biesboer, B. Hansen, and D. Stenlund. 2003. Performance of erosion control products on a highway embankment. *Transactions of the ASAE* 46 (4):1113–1119.

Brix, H. 1999. How 'green' are aquaculture, constructed wetlands and conventional wastewater treatment systems? *Water Science and Technology* 40 (3):45–50.

Buchanan, J. R., D. C. Yoder, H. P. Denton, and J. L. Smoot. 2002. Wood chips as a soil cover for construction sites with steep slopes. *Applied Engineering in Agriculture* 18 (6):679–683.

Demars, K. R., R. P. Long, and J. R. Ives. 2004. Erosion control using wood waste materials. *Compost Science & Utilization* 12 (1):35–47.

Faucette, L. B., C. F. Jordan, L. M. Risse, M. Cabrera, D. C. Coleman, and L. T. West. 2005. Evaluation of stormwater from compost and conventional erosion control practices in construction activities. *Journal of Soil and Water Conservation* 60 (6):288–297.

Glanville, T. D., R. A. Persyn, T. L. Richard, J. M. Laflen, and P. M. Dixon. 2004. Environmental effects of applying composted organics to new highway embankments: Part 2. Water quality. *Transactions of the ASAE* 47 (2):471–478.

Harbor, J. M., J. Synder, and J. Storer. 1995. Reducing nonpoint source pollution from construction sites using rapid seeding and mulching. *Physical Geography* 16 (5):371–388.

Iowa Dept. Natural Resour. 2006. How to Control Streambank Erosion.

Johnson, P. A., R. L. Tereska, and E. R. Brown. 2002. Using technical adaptive management to improve design guidelines for urban instream structures. *Journal of the American Water Resources Association* 38 (4):1143–1152.

Kaufman, M. M. 2000. Erosion control at construction sites: The science-policy gap. *Environmental Management* 26 (1):89–97.

Kochel, R. C., J. R. Miller, M. Lord, and T. Martin. 2005. Geomorphic problems with in-stream structures using natural channel design strategy for stream restoration projects in North Carolina. Paper read at Geol. Soc. Amer. Annual Meeting, at Salt Lake City, UT.

Kozlowski, T. T. 1999. Soil compaction and growth of woody plants. *Scandinavian Journal of Forest Research* 14 (6):596–619.

Krenitsky, E. C., M. J. Carroll, R. L. Hill, and J. M. Krouse. 1998. Runoff and sediment losses from natural and man-made erosion control materials. *Crop Science* 38 (4):1042–1046.

Legret, M., L. Odie, D. Demare, and A. Jullien. 2005. Leaching of heavy metals and polycyclic aromatic hydrocarbons from reclaimed asphalt pavement. *Water Research* 39 (15):3675–3685.

Li, M. H., and K. E. Eddleman. 2002. Biotechnical engineering as an alternative to traditional engineering methods—A biotechnical streambank stabilization design approach. *Landscape and Urban Planning* 60 (4):225–242.

Lye, D. J. 2002. Health risks associated with consumption of untreated water from household roof catchment systems. *Journal of the American Water Resources Association* 38 (5):1301–1306.

Mahler, B. J., P. C. Van Metre, T. J. Bashara, J. T. Wilson, and D. A. Johns. 2005. Parking lot sealcoat: An unrecognized source of urban polycyclic aromatic hydrocarbons. *Environmental Science & Technology* 39 (15):5560–5566.

Park, S. B., and M. Tia. 2004. An experimental study on the water-purification properties of porous concrete. *Cement and Concrete Research* 34 (2):177–184.

Pengchai, P., H. Furumai, and F. Nakajima. 2004. Source apportionment of polycyclic aromatic hydrocarbons in road dust in Tokyo. *Polycyclic Aromatic Compounds* 24 (4–5):773–789.

Persyn, R. A., T. D. Glanville, T. L. Richard, J. M. Laflen, and P. M. Dixon. 2005. Environmental effects of applying composted organics to new highway embankments: Part III. Rill erosion. *Transactions of the ASAE* 48 (5):1765–1772.

Schueler, T. R. 2000. Ditches or biological filters. In *The Practice of Watershed Protection*, edited by T. R. Schueler. Ellicott City, MD: Center for Watershed Protection.

Science and Education Administration. 1978. Predicting Rainfall Erosion Losses: USDA.

Simon, K., and A. Steinemann. 2000. Soil bioengineering: Challenges for planning and engineering. *Journal of Urban Planning and Development—ASCE* 126 (2):89–102.

Sistani, K. R., and D. A. Mays. 2001. Nutrient requirements of seven plant species with potential use in shoreline erosion control. *Journal of Plant Nutrition* 24 (3):459–467.

Soupir, M. L., S. Mostaghimi, A. Masters, K. A. Flahive, D. H. Vaughan, A. Mendez, and P. W. McClellan. 2004. Effectiveness of polyacrylamide (PAM) in improving runoff water quality from construction sites. *Journal of the American Water Resources Association* 40 (1):53–66.

Thaxton, C. S., J. Calantoni, and R. A. McLaughlin. 2004. Hydrodynamic assessment of various types of baffles in a sediment retention pond. *Transactions of the ASAE* 47 (3):741–749.

Thomas, P. R., and G. R. Grenne. 1993. Rainwater quality from different roof catchments. *Water Science Technol.* 28:290–299.

Todd, J., and B. Josephson. 1996. The design of living technologies for waste treatment. *Ecological Engineering* 6 (1–3):109–136.

Tyler, R. 2001. Compost filter berms and blankets take on the silt fence. *Biocycle* 42 (1):26–31.

Valavala, S., F. Montes, and L. M. Haselbach. 2006. Area-rated rational coefficients for Portland cement pervious concrete pavement. *Journal of Hydrologic Engineering* 11 (3):257–260.

CHAPTER 9: DIFFERENT PATHS TO SUSTAINABILITY

Alliance for the Chesapeake Bay. Developing a better watershed: Program aims to build better relations between developers, environmentalists. *The Bay Journal*, 11 (10).

Berger C., and Johnstone Q. 1993. *Land Transfer and Finance: Cases and Materials*, 4th ed. Rockville, MD: Aspen Publishers, Inc.

Builders for the Bay Program, Center for Watershed Protection. Ellicott City, MD. www.cwp.org/builders_for_bay.htm; accessed October 2003.

Dye, P. 2000. "A Breath of Fresh Air." *E Environmental Magazine*. XI (Sept.–Oct., No. 5).

Erhorn, H. "The Ecological Concept. " Fraunhofer Institute for Building Physics, Stuttgart, Germany.

Fillmore, B. 1993. "OMSI exhibit good for environment—and pocketbook." *Daily Journal of Commerce (DJC),* April 20: 1, 23.

Frederick County (MD) Consensus Agreement. 1999. Consensus Recommendations for Fredrick County, MD. Center for Watershed Protection. Ellicott City, MD. www.cwp.org/Frederick.pdf; accessed October 2003.

Hines, S. 2005. "Leftovers: In Washington, D.C., castoff tires and spare dirt have become a skatepark." *Landscape Architecture*, 95 (8): 38–43.

Käpplinger, C. 1998. "Space invaders on the dismal periphery." *Architektur.aktuell.* No. 217-218: 42-45.

Linder L. April 23, 2003. American Institute of Architects (AIA) Development Partner of Longdock at Beacon. Personal Communication.

Natural Lands Trust, Inc. 2001. "Conservation Design versus Typical Cluster Regulations." Available online at www.landchoices.org/GGvsCluster5–15–01.pdf; accessed July 14, 2006.

Natural Lands Trust, Inc. "Growing Greener: Conservation by Design." Available online at www.natlands.org/uploads/document_33200515638.pdf; accessed July 15, 2006.

Office of the Governor of New York. "Governor: $1.8 million for Mid-Hudson parks, preservation," press release, March 26, 2001.

Portland Bureau of Environmental Services, City of Portland, Oregon. 2005. Oregon Museum of Science and Industry (OMSI) Parking Lot Swales. Report. Available online at www.portlandonline.com/shared/cfm/image.cfm?id=78489; accessed July 12, 2006.

Rocky Mountain Institute. 1998. *Green Development: Integrating Ecology and Real Estate.* New York: John Wiley & Sons, Inc.

Schepens, B. 2003. "Park in the Sky." *NYC24,* 3 (2). Available online at www.nyc24.org/2003/issue2/story3/page3.html; accessed Aug. 11, 2006.

Thompson, W. T. 1996. "Let That Soak." *Landscape Architecture,* 86 (11): 60-67.

United Nations Environment Programme. "The Industrial Symbiosis in Kalundborg, Denmark." Environmental Management for Industrial Estates: Information and Training Resources. Available online at www.uneptie.org/pc/ind-estates/casestudies/kalundborg.htm; accessed Aug. 10, 2006.

Index

WILEY BOOKS ON Sustainable Design

For these and other Wiley books on sustainable design, visit www.wiley.com/go/sustainabledesign

Environmental Benefits Statement

This book is printed with soy-based inks on presses with VOC levels that are lower than the standard for the printing industry. The paper, Rolland Enviro 100, is manufactured by Cascades Fine Paper Group and is made from 100 percent postconsumer, de-inked fiber, without chlorine. According to the manufacturer, the following resources were saved by using Rolland Enviro 100 for this book:

Mature trees	Waterborne waste not created	Water flow saved (in gallons)	Atmospheric emissions eliminated	Energy not consumed	Natural gas saved by using biogas
225	103,500 lbs.	153,000	21,470 lbs	259 million BTUs	37,170 cubic feet